A History of Domestic Space

Peter Ward

A History of Domestic Space:
Privacy and the Canadian Home

UBCPress · Vancouver · Toronto

For John Ward, a brother for all seasons.

Printed in Canada on acid-free paper

ISBN 0-7748-0684-2

Canadian Cataloguing in Publication Data

Ward, W. Peter (William Peter), 1943-

A history of domestic space

Includes bibliographical references and index.
ISBN 0-7748-0684-2

1. Dwellings – Canada – History.
2. Architecture, Domestic – Canada – History. 3. Architecture and society – Canada. I. Title.
NA7241.W37 1999   728'.0971
C99-910643-0

This book has been published with the help of a grant from the Humanities and Social Sciences Federation of Canada, using funds provided by the Social Sciences and Humanities Research Council of Canada.

UBC Press acknowledges the financial support of the Government of Canada through the Book Publishing Industry Development Program (BPIDP) for our publishing activities.

Canadä

We also gratefully acknowledge the ongoing support to our publishing program from the Canada Council for the Arts and the British Columbia Arts Council.

Set in Berthold Walbaum and Futura
Printed and bound in Canada by Friesens
Designer: George Vaitkunas
Copy editor: Camilla Jenkins
Proofreader: Darlene Money
Indexer: Annette Lorek

UBC Press
University of British Columbia
6344 Memorial Road
Vancouver, BC V6T 1Z2
(604) 822-5959
Fax: 1-800-668-0821
E-mail: info@ubcpress.ubc.ca
www.ubcpress.ubc.ca

Individualism is a calm and considered feeling which disposes each citizen to isolate himself from the mass of his fellows and withdraw into the circle of family and friends; with this little society formed to his taste, he gladly leaves the greater society to look after itself.

Alexis de Tocqueville, *Democracy in America*, 1835

The skins of houses are shallow things that people are willing to change, but people are most conservative about the spaces they must utilize, and in which they must exist. Build the walls of anything, deck them out with anything, but do not change the arrangement of the rooms or their proportions. In these volumes – bounded by surfaces from which a person's senses rebound to him – his psyche develops; disrupt them, and you disrupt him.

Henry Glassie, 'Folk Art,' 1976

Contents

Acknowledgments

Most books about the past are collaborative efforts and this one is no exception. Over the course of its writing I've enjoyed the generous help of family, friends, and colleagues, to say nothing of a small army of librarians and archivists from coast to coast. The list is too long to include here but I particularly want to thank the following. First and foremost I'm grateful to Pat, Katie, and Anna Ward. Most of what I know about Canadian home life in the late twentieth century I've learned from living with them. They've taken a lively interest in this project and have offered their shrewd appraisals of what I've written as the book proceeded. I'm equally grateful to my good friend and (alas now retired) colleague James Winter. His longstanding interest in the social history of buildings prompted my own, and his comments have made a great difference. Barry Bragg, friend of my youth and aficionado of architectural history, gave me thoughtful advice after reading an early draft. So did Annmarie Adams, whose insights into these matters are far deeper than mine. Eileen Mak and Louise Robert were my eyes for some of the research and Louise doubled as constructive critic at a later stage. Susan Buggey, Heather McAndrew, John O'Brian, Sandra Woolfrey, and Graeme Wynn also offered comments along the way, leaving their mark on these pages as they did. Laura Macleod and Jean Wilson have been shrewd and supportive editors; I very much appreciate their advice and confidence. Camilla Jenkins' sharp pencil has left its mark here too. She has saved me from myself more times than I'd like to admit. Finally, I'm particularly grateful to Peter Milroy for his firm support throughout the life of this study. It's meant a great deal more to me than he knows.

A History of Domestic Space

1 | Housing and Privacy

This is a history of domestic space in Canada. What interests me here is how Canadians have lived in their homes over time. I'm not an historian of architecture but rather a social historian with a longstanding interest in houses. I've lived in several, looked at many more, and read about them for much of my life. Yet much of what I've read on the history of the home has left me vaguely dissatisfied. To me it's always seemed that the genre has viewed dwellings as aesthetic statements much more than as places where people have passed their lives. I've been particularly struck by the lapse that the architect Thomas Markus has pointed out more clearly and succinctly than I ever could. 'Those social historians or critics,' he notes, 'who see an intimate connection between art and society, have left architecture out in the cold. Those architectural historians and critics who treat buildings *as* art objects, have left society out in the cold. What is the origin of this symmetrical silence? If these disciplines do not explain the link between buildings and society, which will do so?'[1] I'm not able to explain why this 'symmetrical silence' exists – that task I leave to others. But in writing this book I've tried to explore the link that Markus refers to, as well as to ponder some of its meanings.

The relationship between the house and the lives it enfolds is complex. Now – as in the past – we choose, build, or alter our dwellings in order to meet some of our needs beyond the basic one of shelter. In turn, because our homes are physical spaces, they impose constraints on us just as they create opportunities for us. In a sense the home is the theatre of our domestic experience, the stage on which we enact much of the long drama of our lives. As a bounded space it sets limits on our actions. No one in a family of five can expect much time alone if they live in a two-room apartment. But it also permits a wide range of actions, depending on its size, technologies, and spatial organization. In an eight-room two-storey townhouse served by fibre optic cable, the five in this family would find many possibilities before them.

While buildings shape human behaviour, human decisions shape buildings. Houses reflect a builder's ideas about what people wish for in a home. A builder might plan to occupy the dwelling herself and so design it with her particular needs in mind. Or he might build for the marketplace in the hope of anticipating what consumers want. Almost inevitably the result will fall short of the mark in one respect or another, and the new occupants will soon begin the task of modifying the building to suit themselves. The first improvements might be only slight, but major renovations are likely to follow in time. Changing family structures, demographic shifts, technological developments, and wayward fashions make old houses obsolete. The only possibilities then are to renovate the building or to tear it down and begin again. Obviously the relationship between homes and home dwellers is an interactive one.

If the house is the stage on which the lives of self and family are displayed, the relations among the actors who inhabit it is one of the drama's great themes. This book has two primary concerns: how spaces in the Canadian home have changed over time, and how family and social relationships have shaped, and been shaped by, these changing spaces. The leitmotif of the discussion is the history of domestic privacy, one of the fundamental elements of daily life for individuals and families, past and present alike.

But privacy is a slippery term and it must be used with some care. Today we talk about privacy in many ways. The law protects our privacy by forbidding others to give out information about us without our consent – private information. It respects our ownership of property – private property. We speak of having personal secrets and conceal our nakedness from strangers – personal privacy. A business owned by an individual or a small group rather than by those who hold publicly traded shares is a private company. Adolescents keep information from their parents in the name of privacy, and families guard their secrets on the same basis.

Privacy may be personal, group, or corporate, and refer to thoughts, places, experiences, or objects.

Notions of privacy have always been contingent, 'constructed,' to use the cultural studies jargon of our universities today. Ideas about the nature of privacy have varied greatly from time to time, place to place, culture to culture. One clue to the relativity of the concept is that the English noun 'privacy,' with all its rich associations, has no equivalent in other major European languages. The French *intimité* is perhaps best translated as it appears – intimacy – while *privé* indicates the individual or personal. No doubt both are elements of privacy but they express only some of the many ideas linked with the English term. The German *zurückgezogenheit* and *privatleben,* literally 'secluded time' and 'private life,' also have related but limited meanings. Italians have solved the problem by importing the word from English but, in this instance too, shorn of most of its nuances.

The concept of privacy involves boundaries if not barriers, lines separating the personal from the public, mine from yours, ours from theirs. Within these boundaries lies the zone of private matters, beyond them the world of general concern. These boundaries may be tangible – walls and fences for example. They may also be customary but nonetheless real, the comfy chair always kept for grandma. Still others may simply be implicit in human relationships, as in the respect we pay by not intruding into the grief of others. Whatever the situation, private matters are invariably thought to be separate from those of broader interest. We speak of them defensively, as being private *from* other things.

Most Canadians also think of privacy as a virtue, something to be valued, defended, perhaps even enlarged. In this sense the concept is permissive or enabling: privacy *to* – to read a book, to bathe, to share the company of family members, to enjoy the ownership of a piece of property. We largely ignore the proximity of the concept of privacy to that of isolation, a form of privacy that we think of in negative terms. The line dividing the two is not always clear and, indeed, may simply express a value judgment about the case at hand. Is isolation merely privacy gone bad?

This book explores two kinds of privacy, that of individuals and that of the family or household. It also considers the two facets of privacy just noted: privacy *from* and privacy *to*. Personal privacy sets the individual apart from the group, creating opportunities for seclusion, times and places to be alone and to pursue one's particular interests. Family privacy draws boundaries between the household and the community. It defends the solidarity of the home and provides a basis for familial relationships. Both forms are intimately involved with the history of the house, for privacy has always been a domestic creature at heart, bound to the homely comforts of the dwelling and to its closed circle of familiar faces.

While we're lingering over meanings we'd do well to pause for a moment over the terms 'house' and 'home.' There's a certain looseness in the ways we commonly use these words, often treating them as synonyms. Yet popular use isn't always so simple. After all, 'home' has much more resonance than 'house,' rich as it is with associations of family and belonging. The marketplace being the arbiter of so many meanings in our society, we shouldn't be surprised that contractors build homes and realtors sell them while, in less market-sensitive contexts, governments provide public housing. In fact, we tacitly accept the notion that a house is simply a building while a home is a domestic setting, filled with human meanings, whose spaces reflect the endless subtleties of everyday family life. I've tried to preserve these distinctions in the discussion that follows.

The forms and settings of dwellings in Canada have altered substantially over the past three centuries. So too have the size and shape of their contents – the household. These changes were the domestic face of the making of modern Canada. From 1700 to the present, the national community evolved from a few scattered European settlements set in a vast and thinly peopled landscape to a postindustrial society spanning the northern half of the continent. Among the most important changes to transform the dominant, European-derived society that is this book's concern, the gradual decline in family size and the general rise of living standards have been central. Both have had profound implications for housing and family life, as well as for the many ties between them.

Over time the changing size, shape, technology, and location of the home have created widely different opportunities for family and personal privacy. Along with major shifts in household composition and family size, these changes have gradually altered the conditions of everyday domestic life. But the pattern of change has been far from uniform. Women have experienced it in different ways from men, children from adults, country people from city dwellers, the poor from the rich, Newfoundlanders from British Columbians, and so on. The nature, meaning, and experience of privacy in Canadian history has varied enormously over the past 300 years. In what follows I want to explore some of these experiences and meanings, and to reflect on their implications for family and social life, past and present.

2 | Interiors

Little House, Big House

The one-room dwelling is the oldest house type in Canada. It long predates the coming of Europeans, as the archaeological record shows. It was the first shelter built by the earliest European migrants, and it persisted on every frontier from the early seventeenth to the late twentieth centuries. It flourishes in our cities today as the studio apartment. Over time the simple single-room home has proved endlessly adaptable to the basic need for shelter. In most cases these have been temporary buildings, hastily built to meet immediate needs. Usually they were enlarged or replaced as soon as settler families could afford it. Still, the small dwelling probably remained the dominant form of housing in Canada from the earliest years of settlement until the mid-nineteenth century, and well into the twentieth in some parts of the country. Despite the vast outdoor spaces surrounding them, until quite recently most Canadian families lived their domestic lives in small, confined places.

Unfortunately the early history of the house in Canada is rather sketchy. The first dwellings were made of wood and have long since vanished. Archaeology and the archives have told us a bit about them, but we'll never know very much about housing in Canada before the eighteenth century. For this reason the story of the Canadian home is essentially that of the past three centuries.

The first homes we know at all were those of the rural St Lawrence Valley. Some were built on the Ile d'Orléans, one of the earliest areas of European settlement in Quebec. The Maison Mourier is probably the oldest example, a one-room dwelling built in 1690 and measuring sixteen by twenty feet (five by six metres) (Figure 1). This small space housed a fireplace, a bread oven, a cool storage space for dairy produce, and a stairway to the attic –

presumably sleeping quarters for at least some of the residents – as well as an open area for whatever furnishings they may have had. The Mourier house was something of an exception because it was built of stone. No doubt this is why we know about it today. By the end of the French regime in 1760 most farmhouses on the Ile d'Orléans – as everywhere else in New France – were small, one-storey, one- or two-room wooden dwellings put up by their occupants. They were simply built and furnished, and usually used the attic as added sleeping space. Some may even have sheltered the family's large domestic animals in the cold months of the year.[2]

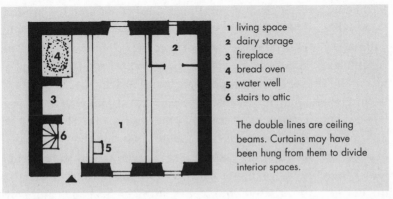

1 living space
2 dairy storage
3 fireplace
4 bread oven
5 water well
6 stairs to attic

The double lines are ceiling beams. Curtains may have been hung from them to divide interior spaces.

1. Plan for the one-room Maison Mourier, Quebec, 1690.

The early homes of Acadia were similar. We know almost nothing about those built before the expulsions of the 1750s, but Captain John MacDonald described the returned Acadians' dwellings in a report to the governor of Cape Breton Island in the last years of the century:

The premises of every one seem to be a house from 18 to 25 feet long & as many in breadth without porch or partition but the outer door opening immediately into the sole room. There are generally two doors, the one being that which is used. The chimney ... is in the remotest part from the door. The Beds are on both sides of the house from chimney to the doors. In the end of the house opposite to the chimney, the pots and water vessels lie on the floor and the Milk & Milk vessels are disposed of on shelves, together with their bowls, muggs &c: As they all sleep, eat, cook, smoke, wash, &c: in this house or room, I need not say it must look black & dirty enough particularly as the houses are now old. ... I had almost forgot to mention that their houses have a cellar under the ground for the roots &c to which they descend by a trap door in the floor.[3]

The small homes in the first British settlements of Atlantic Canada were very little different: one- and two-room cabins, perhaps with attic sleeping lofts for children.[4]

The Newfoundland tilt was the simplest of all variants of the frontier home. It normally consisted of a single room with walls formed by a rectangle of vertical poles buried end first in a trench. One wall was slightly higher than the one facing it, and the walls connecting these two were made of successively shorter poles. The result was then covered by a sloping roof with a hole in one end to let out the smoke from the open hearth fire inside. The tilt provided basic shelter, often only seasonally, from its introduction in the six-teenth century throughout much of the nineteenth. The Anglican missionary Edward Wix recalled one he visited on the Isle of Valen in 1835, 'the dimensions of which were only 12 feet by 10 feet and I found living in it a man and his wife – the master and mistress of the house – two married daughters with their husbands and chil-dren, amounting, in all, to fifteen souls.'[5]

The British traveller John Howison noted the slightly sturdier dwellings of frontier Upper Canada when passing through the province in 1820. The usual log and plank house, he observed, measured sixteen by eighteen feet (four by five metres) and con-tained only one room. Howison believed that the pioneer should have higher priorities than domestic comfort when setting up a farm: 'The farmer ought to pay little attention to his dwelling-house, until he has provided a safe depository for his grain, and a warm shed to shelter his cattle. In Upper Canada, a miserable hovel is often seen in the midst of fruitful fields and fine orchards, forming a singular contrast with the handsome barn, which its owner has wisely spent his first gains in erecting.'[6] Otto Sierich's undated sketch of a pioneer cabin provides a glimpse of the small and simply furnished interiors that Howison saw on his travels (Figure 2).

2. Undated sketch of the interior of a pioneer cabin.

The first homes built by prairie settlers a century later – the temporary log huts, sod houses, and shacks – differed little in spatial terms. Cheaply and quickly built even by hands with few skills, they were by far the most common house forms during the early settlement years. In 1911, as the great wave of migration to the prairie region crested, almost half of all dwellings in Alberta and Saskatchewan had only one or two rooms – a sharp contrast to long-settled Ontario and Quebec, where only one home in twenty-five was this small. In some prairie ethnic communities the proportion was larger still. In 1917, two-thirds of the early Ukrainian settlers in Alberta lived in one- or two-room homes, patterned on designs brought from the homeland. Normally these buildings were only intended for short-term use. Sod huts lasted a season or two at best, while shacks knocked together from cheap machine-made building materials offered poor protection against the bitter prairie winter. Soon their owners either improved them or abandoned them to chickens.[7]

In northern Canada the one- or two-room house persisted into the second half of the century. The two-room dwelling shown in

3. Interior of a one-room house in Fort St James, British Columbia, c. 1950.

Figure 3 reveals the classic form, a small, rough lumber building warmed by a central space heater and lighted by a mantle lamp. Though the photograph was taken in Fort St James, BC, in 1950 it could have come from almost anywhere in Canada from the late seventeenth century onward. When compared with the early-nineteenth-century Sierich sketch, for example, only the lamp, the couple's clothing, and a few domestic articles betray its mid-twentieth-century origins. The Inuit family from Inuvik, NWT, shown in a 1959 photograph, lived in a single room, in this case with electric lighting (Figure 4). Mr Dick, the chief wage earner, worked for the federal Department of Public Works though he continued to hunt, trap, and fish. In some respects the Dicks were atypical Canadians for they were members of a community in transition from the northern hunting and gathering economy of time immemorial to the consumer society of the late twentieth century. But their living space also linked them with another centuries-old tradition of frontier life in Canada, that of the pioneer home.

4. An Inuit family in their one-room house at
Inuvik, Northwest Territories, 1959.

The small house was also a pervasive urban form from the eighteenth century on. We see an early example in the surviving floor plan for one of the first tracts of workers' housing in Quebec (Figure 5). Dated 1801, it sketches the outline of a six-unit row of simple three-room homes attached to the winter drying house of the Bécancour Hemp Works. The units themselves were small (fifteen by thirty French feet, or five by ten metres) and the use of the rooms unspecified – though the oven in one surely designates the kitchen. Homes like these were common in French Canadian towns and cities during the first half of the nineteenth century. We know that most artisans' and labourers' families in the Quebec City suburb of Saint-Roch, for example, generally lived in one to three rooms.[8]

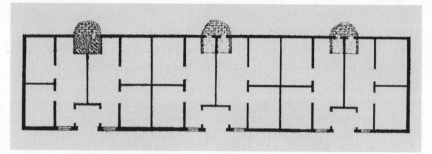

5. Detail of plan for Bécancour Hemp Works row housing for workers, Quebec, c. 1801.

From midcentury, however, the amount of space in urban dwellings began to increase. The average size of Montreal homes increased from 4.6 to 5.7 rooms during the last forty years of the nineteenth century, when the city's population trebled and home building expanded rapidly to meet strong demand. Even in the new industrial villages of rural Quebec the traditional one-room house gave way to larger dwellings during these years. Still, in Quebec as elsewhere the small urban home remained a feature of most labouring people's lives well into the twentieth century. A survey of Montreal's low-income housing in 1937 revealed that, of over 4,000 homes inspected, one-quarter still had no more than three rooms. At this time the official rate of overcrowding (one or more persons per room, counting all rooms except storage and attics) in urban English Canada seems to have ranged between 10 and 20 percent.[9]

But increasingly the small city dwelling came to be regarded as a social problem – linked with poverty and its many attendant ills. In fact by the early twentieth century the small home had taken on a pathological meaning and attracted powerful opponents. No longer the intimate setting of everyday family life, it now was considered the prime site of urban distress and squalor. Civic reformers and public health activists fought hard against small dwellings. Their most potent weapons were standards of residential density and sanitary practice, which they themselves had defined. Judged by these measures the housing conditions common in earlier generations were no longer acceptable. In 1912, inspectors from the Toronto Department of Health announced the discovery of 4,500 overcrowded houses in the city, some with families of six or more living in single rooms. A century before who would have thought this a problem? By most contemporary European standards the proportion of Canadians housed in overcrowded dwellings was small indeed. In Paris at the turn of the century, for example, at least a quarter of the population lived two or more to a room. Variation was widespread even within the same nation. Half the population of Scotland occupied one- or two-room dwellings on the eve of the First World War, while in England and Wales the proportion was only 7 percent.[10]

Of course there were large homes too, even in the frontier years – spacious dwellings with several rooms usually identified with specific functions. In fact the early European settlers established an inequality of domestic space in their communities during the first years of settlement. Colonial elites built houses reflecting their claims to status, wealth, and dignity while the less privileged built with an eye to utility, cost, and imitation. The social hierarchy was endlessly reproduced in a hierarchy of spaciousness. The homes of the wealthy defined norms of comfort and roominess that other families strove to emulate as best they could.

We see a striking example of spatial plenty in the domestic life of Quebec City businessman John William Woolsey and his family, best known to us as subjects of a celebrated portrait by William Berczy painted in 1809 (Plate 1). At the end of his long life Woolsey drew up a table of the thirteen houses he and his family had lived in from the time of his marriage in 1797. He listed their rooms, their uses, their lengths and widths. Why he did this is not at all obvious but his list provides an exceptionally clear view of the spaces a prosperous Canadian family occupied during the first half of the nineteenth century.

The Woolseys spent the first twenty years of married life in three large houses in the old city. Each had spacious drawing and dining rooms, a main bedroom, one bedroom for their three sons, another for their only daughter, a spare bedroom, and a nursery that doubled as a second spare bedroom. Each also included a large kitchen, a pantry, a store room, and a maid's room, while the kitchen doubled as the manservant's room. The total floor area of each of the three houses ranged between 2,200 and 2,800 square feet (200 and 260 square metres), about the size of a good-sized suburban house today. Thereafter the family grew and shrank as marriage, childbirth, and death expanded and thinned its ranks. Most of the Woolseys' later dwellings were a little smaller, the smallest a house they moved to after two sons had died and their only daughter had left home to marry. It was a two-bedroom house with the same public and service rooms as their former homes, plus additional chambers for two servants. Like their earlier dwellings, all of the Woolseys' later houses included rooms for specific purposes. When he drew up this chart at the age of eighty-five Woolsey was a lonely widower and all of his children had died as well. In reduced financial circumstances he was renting the last of the homes on his list, perhaps residing with his son's widow and children. Its living space totalled 2,000 square feet (185 square metres) and, apart from a missing pantry, it had the same number of rooms with the same basic functions as the house he and his bride had first shared more than half a century earlier.[11]

The Woolseys' homes were far from exceptional. The large house boasting a number of rooms with specialized functions was common in early British America. A few dating from the pre- and immediate post-Conquest years were scattered throughout Quebec. Many more were built in the province during the early and mid-nineteenth century, when the accumulation of wealth from commerce and seigneurial landholding created a growing moneyed class with a taste for large, handsome dwellings. Some were commissioned by members of the colony's British elite, who shared their culture's preference for spacious country homes. But French Canada's wealthy residents were equally attracted to the big house. Many of Quebec's most imposing seigneurial residences date from the 1800s – the nationalist politician Louis Joseph Papineau's seigneurial manor house 'Montebello' at Petite Natione, for instance. Another, more modest example is the one-storey wooden house built for the painter Antoine Plamondon at Pointe aux Trembles in 1846 and shown on p. 84. It measured fifty-five by thirty feet (seventeen by nine metres) and included seven rooms as well as an attached atelier.[12]

Some of the New England settlers in Nova Scotia built large dwellings during the late eighteenth century. The Simeon Perkins house in Liverpool is perhaps the best-known example, a small cottage that grew over time with his family's changing needs and rising prosperity. Perkins, a merchant, office holder, and local notable, as well as eighteenth-century English Canada's most prominent diarist, left us a rich record of the history of his house.[13] Like many eighteenth-century dwellings it grew by stages. It was erected in 1766 as a modest, three-room, single-floor dwelling with a sleeping attic upstairs. Over the next quarter century the Perkins family enlarged their home twice to accommodate an expanding family of eight, first by extending it across the frontage to add new bedrooms and a larger kitchen, then by adding yet another kitchen and attic in a rear wing that formed the stem of the home's new 'T' shape. By the time Perkins died in 1812 the house seems to have grown to at least ten rooms.

Many more of Nova Scotia's stately old homes date from the years just after the turn of the century, when colonial fortunes wrung from commerce and land found formal expression in the gracious neoclassical residences of the era. Acacia Grove at Starrs Point in the Annapolis Valley is a case in point, a three-storey, twelve-room, classically styled brick dwelling measuring forty by fifty-two feet (twelve by sixteen metres), built for a successful Halifax merchant during the 1810s. Nor were large dwellings the preserve of only the wealthy. Spacious, multiroom houses, designed in a range of imported and adapted styles, were common in the Maritimes from the late eighteenth century. Early Upper Canada had the same array of large and medium-sized homes by the time the early pioneer years had passed. In the Niagara district, for example, a number of craftsmen and retail merchants built large one-and-a-half-storey frame houses well before the War of 1812.[14]

The Question of Crowding

From the standpoint of domestic space and its uses, the fact that both small and large houses have a long history in Canada is less important than knowing what proportions of the population lived in differing settings. After all, a small home might be spacious enough for one or two people while a big one could well be crowded if the household were large. We have no way of knowing if all eight Woolseys in the 1809 portrait (John William, his wife Julie Lemoine, their four children, and his wife's mother and brother) lived together. But assuming they did and adding the two live-in servants that middle-class families often employed, the house they occupied when their portrait was painted had one room per person – with another left over for Brador, the dog.

Of course the well-to-do Woolseys enjoyed the luxury of far more household space than most of their contemporaries. Unfortunately we don't know very much about how most Canadian families fitted into their homes until toward the end of the nineteenth century, and what little we know comes from widely scattered sources. Best known is Herbert Ames's late-nineteenth-century muck-raking classic *The City below the Hill*, a social survey of Montreal slum life that set out in search of overcrowding but had some trouble finding much. A recent study of working-class family life in early industrial Montreal also concluded that overcrowding was uncommon, though observing that many families shared their modest living spaces with relations or other families at some point in their lives. Such studies, however, tend to emphasize the lot of the working poor and don't tell us much about broader conditions. One exception is the much-studied city of Hamilton, where the ratio of residents to rooms declined steadily for all classes from the 1870s.[15]

The national census began to count the number of rooms in each dwelling in 1891 but the information wasn't thought important enough to publish at the time. Still, in their raw form the data offer us a chance to look a bit more closely at the fit between families and their living spaces in the late nineteenth century. I've used the census manuscripts to look at the housing conditions of four towns in that year: Lunenburg in Nova Scotia, Joliette in Quebec, Perth in eastern Ontario, and Calgary in Alberta. Together they provide some impressions of the range of spaces available inside the Canadian dwelling of that era. Lunenburg was a fishing and ship-building community founded well over a century earlier; its fortunes had been on the wane since the golden years of midcentury Maritime prosperity. Joliette, established during the 1820s, was a small industrial and service centre in the St Lawrence Valley surrounded by a prosperous farming region. First settled at the end of the Napoleonic wars, Perth, too, was a small manufacturing and service centre, though distant from Toronto and thus from the dynamic core of Ontario's late Victorian industrial growth. Calgary, in contrast, was a new prairie town, not much more than a police post a decade earlier, summoned to urban greatness only by the arrival of the Canadian Pacific Railway in 1883. The four towns had rather different economies and growth patterns so we shouldn't consider them typical. For our purposes they merely illustrate some of the diverse housing conditions found in late-nineteenth-century Canada.

A glance at Table 1 reveals some sharp contrasts in housing conditions in the four communities. Most important, there was a marked difference in the number of families per house. In Calgary, Joliette, and Perth there were enough freestanding dwellings to go round and almost every family occupied their own, while in Lunenburg a third of all buildings sheltered more than one household. This isn't to say that these families lived together. Normally they occupied separate rooms or apartments within the same structures.

Table 1

Housing conditions in four Canadian towns, 1891

	Population	Number of households	Number of houses	Average household size* (persons)	Median house size (rooms)	Population in less than one room per person (%)	Houses with more than one family (%)
Calgary	3,876	793	757	4.2	4	55	5
Joliette	3,372	771	771	4.2	4	42	0
Lunenburg	4,894	987	746	5.0	7	47	32
Perth	3,314	662	657	5.0	6	31	1

*Barracks, boarding houses, convents, hotels, seminaries, etc. omitted.
Source: Canada, Manuscript Census, 1891, Lunenburg, Nova Scotia; Joliette, Quebec; Perth, Ontario; and Calgary, NWT.

The number of rooms per dwelling varied widely in these places, from as few as one to as many as fifteen and more. The Lunenburg homes were rather larger on average than those in Perth and both were significantly roomier than houses in the other two towns. The average number of residents per home varied as well; the two communities with more spacious dwellings also had larger households. As for crowding, between a third and a half of each town's population lived in overcrowded homes – if by that term we mean the generally accepted late-nineteenth-century social reformers' index of less than one room per person. Whether these people thought of themselves as overcrowded is quite another question. Views about such matters are quite subjective and they've varied considerably over the years. In late-nineteenth-century Britain, for example, two or more per room was the generally accepted definition of an overcrowded home.

Overcrowding had much less to do with small houses per se than it did with large families. For the most part, those who lived in the most crowded quarters were either middle-aged couples with numerous children or blended families created in the wake of widowhood or similar misfortune. Usually the wage earners in these families had modest jobs if they had any at all. Frontier Calgary was something of a special case. The recent rapid growth of the city had come at the cost of a great deal of improvised housing. Over 40 percent of the city's dwelling stock had three or fewer rooms. While some of these were home to but one or two residents, others housed large families – up to nine per room in some cases.

At the other end of the spectrum were those who lived in spatial abundance. A few were the rich and powerful who built domestic monuments to their own magnificence. In pioneer Calgary the nine-member household of William Pearce – husband, wife, four children, and three servants – lived in a twenty-three-room mansion just a stone's throw from the small shacks that overflowed with the city's most recent arrivals.[16] (Pearce was superintendent of mines in the Department of the Interior and probably the most powerful civil servant in the early prairie West.) But far more often those who lived spaciously were those who lived alone. The greatest number were older widows or widowers, women and men who had probably moved into large homes when their families needed the space and then stayed behind, predeceased by their spouses, when their children left to set up households of their own. No doubt they too were better off than their least privileged neighbours, but not necessarily a great deal richer. These weren't communities with great extremes of wealth. (Even Pearce was just a civil servant, and he was probably the last one in the West to live in such a grand manner.) What separated the few who enjoyed the luxury of space from the many who did not was as much their stage of life as any other factor – though no doubt a measure of good fortune was often involved as well.

We begin to get a broader picture of the number of rooms per dwelling in Canada from 1911, when the national census began publishing these statistics. Figure 6 provides a brief summary of national patterns in the twentieth century. It illustrates the trend toward moderately sized houses before the 1960s, and the shift back toward bigger dwellings over the past four decades. The small home, meanwhile, has been in decline throughout most of the century. The graph also indicates that Canadian household size declined by 50 percent between 1881 and 1991. Thus, on average at

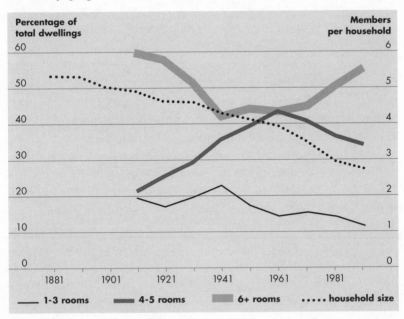

6. Rooms per dwelling and household size, Canada, 1881-1991.

least, the amount of room space available to each Canadian has grown dramatically over time. Nevertheless, the graph conceals the great regional variation during the early part of the century. Large homes were much more common in Ontario and the Maritimes, while small ones were heavily concentrated in the West. But over time these differences have shrunk, and all parts of the country have come to share more or less the same range of house forms, at least in terms of average room numbers.

Averages conceal at least as much as they reveal, particularly when it comes to understanding the living conditions of the disadvantaged. In our century the housing standards of the poor have come to be regarded as an important measure of community well-being. During the late nineteenth and early twentieth centuries urban reformers defined the concept of overcrowding, then linked it with low wages and high population growth in Canada's swelling cities. Though Ames found little classic overcrowding in working-class Montreal around 1900 it certainly was a problem there and elsewhere at other times. In fact, housing densities have varied dramatically from time to time and place to place, especially for families living on the social margins.[17]

In terms of domestic space, those housed in crowded dwellings continued to live in the same types of settings as earlier generations. The impoverished Toronto family in Figure 7, a rare early-twentieth-century photograph of an inner city interior, is a striking example. The three in the photo lived in a single, multipurpose room heated by a central stove, much like the pioneer family sketched in Figure 2. Taken in 1911 by a city health official, this picture was a weapon in the early-twentieth-century campaign for public health reform. Yet whatever the photographer's polemical intent, the image clearly reveals a nameless family living well outside minimum civic housing standards of the time. Like many of the nation's poor, these three hadn't benefited from the gradual rise in living standards that had slowly improved the national housing stock over the previous century.

The persistence of traditional domestic spaces in rural communities was equally striking, as can be seen in the simple 1920s Quebec farm home interior depicted in Figure 8. While we'll never know what lay behind the camera, the scene before it was as old as

7. Toronto slum interior, 1911.

8. *Winding the Warp*, Quebec, 1920s,
MP-1992.10.4.

rural Quebec itself. The woman winding the warp was involved in an ancient feminine task, one of the many longstanding contributions women made to the household economy whether their woollen goods were used at home or sold for cash. The room itself obviously served several functions: production, leisure (the chair), and food preparation (the cupboard, counter, and pots to the right). This scene was a far cry from the urban poverty glimpsed in the previous figure but the spaces themselves are strikingly similar. In neither case do we see the domestic amenities and spaces that growing numbers of early-twentieth-century Canadians had come to accept as their due.

The Organization of Household Space

As long as homes had only a few rooms these served many functions during the daily round of family life: cooking, eating, food production, craft manufacturing, sleeping. Kitchens were a partial exception, at least where they existed as a separate space, but they too often served many additional purposes as they still do today in some parts of the country. It remains common in rural and small-town Canada, for example, to entertain close family friends in the kitchen. The British traveller John Lambert, who passed through Canada in the early years of the nineteenth century, noticed that while some Canadian houses had only one or two rooms, most – at least those of the better sort of farmer – consisted of four. From what he could tell, the kitchen was the room with the chimney and all the remainder were bedrooms. 'No matter how many apartments there are in a house, they are seldom without one or two beds in each, according to the size of the family,' he remarked.[18] Probably their occupants lived more comfortably than many urban residents – the workers of Saint-Roch noted above, for example, whose homes were somewhat smaller. Throughout their work and domestic lives most families, large and small, lived in tight quarters. At times rooms might be partitioned with curtains to create some personal space, but it was almost impossible to be alone in such circumstances.

Larger dwellings offered more flexibility and so, not surprisingly, the use of particular spaces for specific purposes developed first in bigger homes. In the late eighteenth century the large

French-Canadian rural house gradually divided into three areas, one for everyday family life and domestic tasks, a second for formal occasions, and a third for sleeping. Daily life most often unfolded in the *salle commune* (common room), which generally doubled as the kitchen. Bedrooms slowly made their appearance at this time, all rooms usually connecting directly with one another. The eighteenth-century Paradis house of Charlesbourg, Quebec, illustrates the type, with its sleeping rooms ranged along the back wall of the dwelling, their doors leading into one another as well as into the parlour and kitchen (Figure 9). During the first half of the nine- teenth century further refinements occurred: the development of a separate summer kitchen, the emergence of the salon, or parlour (at the expense of the large kitchen, once the centre of daily life in the household but now shrunk in the face of claims for a more formal way of living), the introduction of corridors to separate rooms from one another, and finally the removal of bedrooms to the greater seclusion of a second floor.[19]

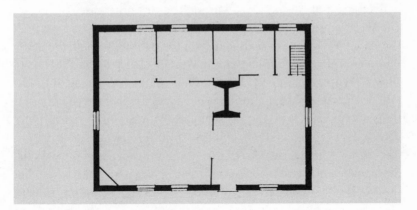

9. Detail of plan for Paradis House, Charlesbourg, Quebec, late eighteenth century.

Big houses in English Canada passed through much the same transition during the nineteenth century. Functionally their interior spaces became more specialized, while the lines between zones of relative privacy became more sharply inscribed. A one-and-a-half-storey Loyalist house built on the Niagara peninsula around the beginning of the century offers an early example. The sketchy plan in Figure 10 was submitted with a claim for losses from property damaged during the American invasion in 1813, and as a result it contains only a small bit of information. But it indicates the number, shape, and position of the rooms, if not their precise uses. (Some bedrooms were probably located upstairs in a half storey, though these aren't shown in the plan.) Numbers apart, the most obvious feature of several rooms is the fact that they spanned the dwelling from front to back, on either side of a broad corridor that bisected the house.

The so-called Georgian plan was another increasingly popular layout during the first half of the new century, at least among well-to-do British colonists. Acacia Grove, a large early-nineteenth-century Starrs Point, Nova Scotia, house, is a fine example (Figure 11).[20] The symmetrical arrangement of the rooms on each floor expressed traditional classical ideals of harmony and balance. The practice of identifying rooms with particular purposes (drawing room, library, dining room) and the separation of the private aspects of domestic life from those more widely shared (sleeping and dressing from conversing and eating) spread as the century progressed.

We see one of the nineteenth-century high points of the genre in the Wilton Crescent house designed for the wealthy Toronto financier, politician, and art patron George William Allan during the early 1850s (Figures 12 to 14). The main floor of this handsome, if ostentatious, house featured a number of rooms for specific social functions, as well as a service area set apart from the public parts of the dwelling. Sleeping, bathing, and dressing were removed to the second storey, with quarters for female servants again placed to one side. Storage, heating, and male servants were relegated to the basement.

We need to read architectural plans with some caution. They're statements of intent, not practice, so they don't necessarily indicate how residents lived in their homes day by day. Not only that but owners commonly renovate their homes to take account of their evolving needs. This has been particularly true of the large dwellings of the rich, so often rendered démodé by changing tastes and shifting neighbourhood preferences, and so easily subdivided into apartments when a once fashionable district loses its cachet. Still, floor plans offer us at least a rough guide to how homes in earlier times were used, and we can accept them as a somewhat flexible indication of the domestic spaces our ancestors occupied.

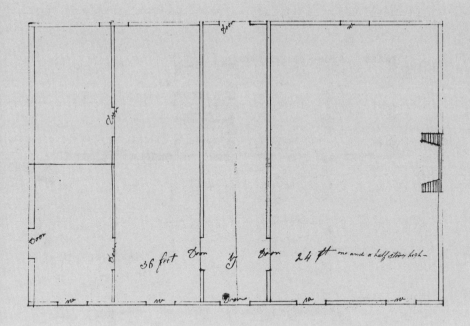

10. Plan for early-nineteenth-century Loyalist house on the Niagara peninsula.

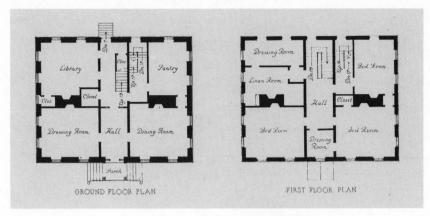

11. Acacia Grove, an early-nineteenth-century house in Starrs Point, Nova Scotia, illustrates the popular Georgian plan.

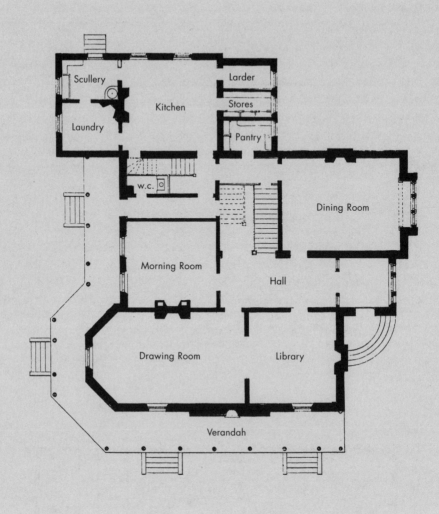

12. Wilton Crescent house designed for the wealthy Toronto financier, politician, and art patron George William Allan during the early 1850s, plan of ground floor.

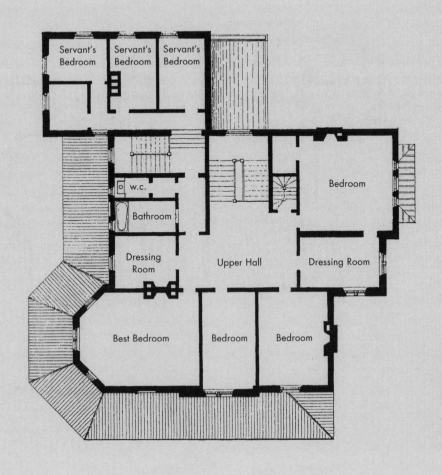

Servant's
Bedroom

Servant's
Bedroom

Servant's
Bedroom

w.c.

Bathroom

Bedroom

Dressing
Room

Upper Hall

Dressing Room

Best Bedroom

Bedroom

Bedroom

13. Wilton Crescent house, 1850s, plan
of upper floor.

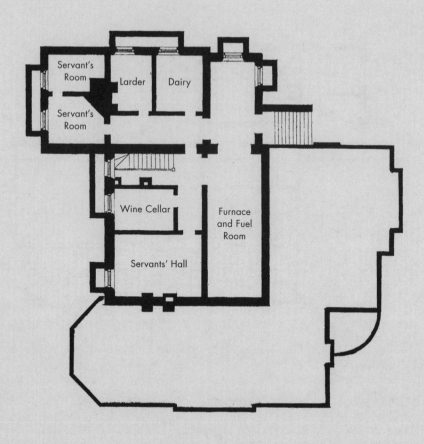

14. Wilton Crescent house, 1850s, plan of basement.

As the century progressed some of the most common housing forms became highly standardized, among them the urban row house, whose roots lay in Great Britain. The English row house was one of many cultural forms transported to North America on the flood tide of British migration during the nineteenth century. It flourished in urban places on both sides of the border. We find many examples in Kingston, Toronto, and the English-speaking parts of Montreal from at least the 1830s and, in fact, they were common in most colonial cities.[21] Like the large nineteenth-century homes we've noted, the row house separated the rooms accessible to guests from those intended for household members. On the main floor the front door opened into a vestibule that led, in turn, to a hallway along one side of the building as well as to stairs to the upper floor or floors. Along the other side of the house the drawing room or parlour, the dining room, and the kitchen ranged one behind the other from front to back, each accessible either from the hall or from the adjacent rooms. Upstairs lay the bed and bath rooms. This spatial arrangement was almost universal in the row house. More substantial and opulent versions had more and larger rooms, and often included a third storey, but the form itself was common across the housing spectrum. Figures 15 to 17 and Figure 18 offer contrasting examples from the late Victorian era, the one of comfortable middle-class homes on Toronto's Jarvis Street, the other of working-class family dwellings in the same city.

The dominant housing type in Montreal between 1850 and 1930 was the 'plex' – the two-storey working-class duplex and the three-storey triplex, which came later. These low-cost innovations in house form were shaped by local peculiarities in housing by-laws, the shape and size of building lots, and market pressures created by the city's low-wage economy. They were quickly adopted in other industrializing Quebec cities, a form of popular housing unique to the province. The dwellings themselves varied a good deal in size, arrangement, and number of rooms.[22] The sample in Figure 19, from a 1937 survey of housing, shows a range from simple two-room suites to six-room dwellings large enough to include salons, bedrooms, dining rooms, and kitchens. Often these dwellings were long and narrow, their rooms placed in a single row from front to back.[23] In some cases interior chambers had no windows because

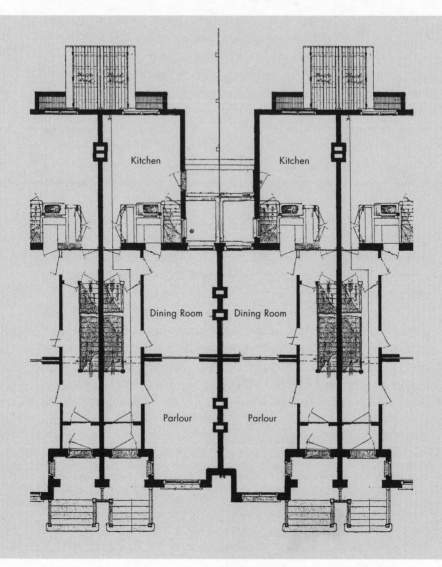

15. Row house, Jarvis Street, Toronto, 1887, plan of ground floor.

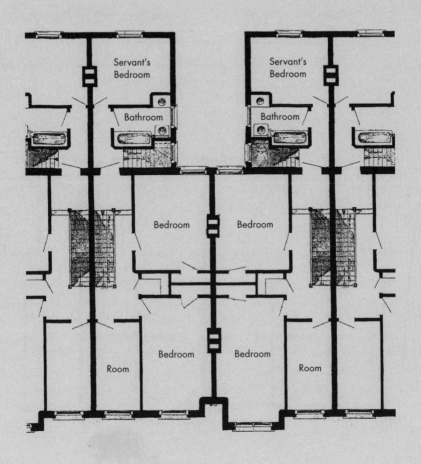

16. Row house, Jarvis Street, Toronto, 1887, plan of chamber floor.

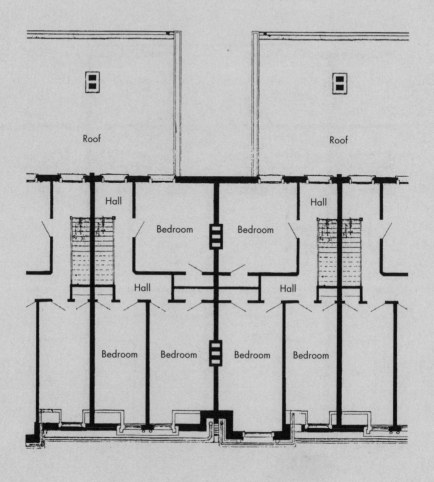

17. Row house, Jarvis Street, Toronto, 1887, plan of attic floor.

18. (facing page) Detail of plan for row houses proposed for working-class families, 1905.

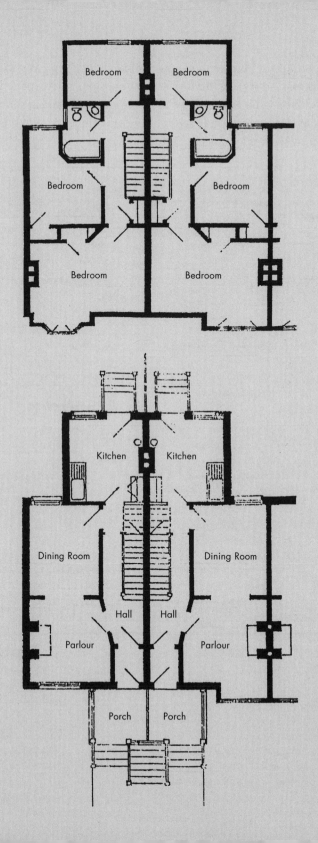

the buildings abutted houses on either side. Typically they lacked corridors as well, a luxury when interior space was scarce, and thus the rooms led directly into one another. But the larger units revealed the same clear separation of rooms by function then common in houses across the country.

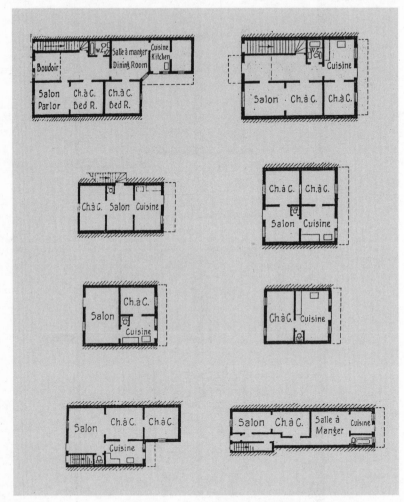

19. Montreal housing survey showing typical late-nineteenth-century single-floor dwellings.

After the turn of the twentieth century the rigidities of the nineteenth-century interior plan began to relax. In large part this was due to the growing American influence on Canadian home design. The architectural historian Vincent Scully long ago revealed that a distinctive style of domestic architecture emerged in the eastern United States during the middle decades of the nineteenth century, one marked by a freer, more open use of interior space.[24] Though its roots lay in the 'high' architecture of the period – the fruit of unions between celebrated architects and wealthy patrons – in time it exerted a powerful influence on popular housing as well.

The so-called open plan, which began to evolve in middle-class American suburban housing during the 1880s, blurred distinctions formerly drawn between the various public rooms of the dwelling. Larger, more inclusive spaces replaced the older pattern of smaller rooms with precisely identified functions, creating open areas for the many activities of everyday family life. In some instances walls were abolished, in others shrunk to archways (often with glass or sliding doors) that retained the symbolism of room functions while permitting more flexibility in their uses.[25] Generally, the public rooms were linked in this way while kitchens, bedrooms, and bathrooms retained their separate identities. The slow spread of central heating also encouraged acceptance of the open plan by making it possible to heat larger interior spaces. In fact the new open plan represented a modified form of the traditional small home, with its characteristic multiple uses of a few rooms.

American open plan home designs had a major impact on English-Canadian housing from the turn of the twentieth century on. Cheap and popular house plans – widely available from newspapers, magazines, and pattern books – provided one point of entry, prefabricated housing a second, and contractors and carpenters a third. Architects often incorporated open plan principles into the homes they designed for the well-to-do. The open plan home spread quickly during the great building boom of the decade before the First World War, when Canada's population grew by a third. Because it encouraged more efficient use of space – by eliminating corridors for example – it trimmed construction costs. It usually also featured built-in cupboards, shelves, and benches, which avoided the need for some large furniture pieces. These efficiencies made the open plan particularly suitable for small dwellings, built in large numbers after the turn of the century. It was especially well adapted to the housing needs of western Canada, where the phenomenal population growth of the period created a heavy demand for small, inexpensive homes.

The bungalow embodied the open plan interior in its simplest, most popular form. While this house type has a long international history, the Canadian version was based on California prototypes developed at the turn of the century. The Craftsman or California bungalow, as it came to be known, was the quintessential twentieth-century American suburban home. As Anthony King, one of its most persuasive historians has put it, 'the development of the small, cheap, yet none the less attractive and individual bungalow was to extend the rustic suburban ideal to millions. It embodied a form of modern popular architecture, conferring the respectability, privacy and sense of territorial possession sought by an aspiring middle class. For an increasing number of people it became their main symbol of home, the psychic fulfilment of the American dream.'[26] Scully has noted the links between mid-nineteenth-century innovations in American domestic architecture and the enormously popular Craftsman home of the early twentieth century. But we shouldn't lose sight of another important influence on the bungalow style, the British Arts and Crafts movement, whose commitment to natural and organic form also left its imprint on the design of interior spaces.

The California bungalow arrived in Canada by way of Vancouver and Victoria and quickly spread – suitably modified for the rigours of the Canadian climate – throughout the West during the great prewar building boom. While the single-floor version of about 1,000 square feet, or 90 square metres, was by far the most common, larger one-and-a-half- and two-storey adaptations were also popular. Bungalows were normally laid out on an open plan, their living and dining areas grouped either in one room or in two rooms divided symbolically. They often lacked vestibules, parlours, and pantries, kept corridors to a minimum, and used built-in features to increase living space (Figure 20).[27] More elaborate houses often preserved those traditional features abandoned in the quest for efficiencies in smaller houses but retained the innovative elements of the new open plan. As we can see in Figure 21, the architect who designed this three-storey, six-bedroom middle-class home in Kingston in 1922 planned a large, contiguous open space linking the hall, living room, dining room, and sun room of the house.

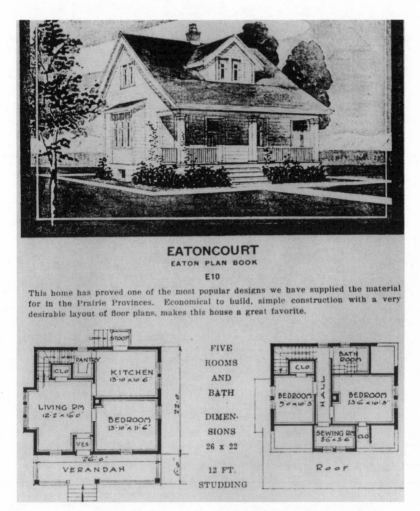

EATONCOURT
EATON PLAN BOOK
E10

This home has proved one of the most popular designs we have supplied the material for in the Prairie Provinces. Economical to build, simple construction with a very desirable layout of floor plans, makes this house a great favorite.

FIVE
ROOMS
AND
BATH

DIMEN-
SIONS
26 x 22

12 FT.
STUDDING

20. Plan for one-and-a-half storey house, 1919.

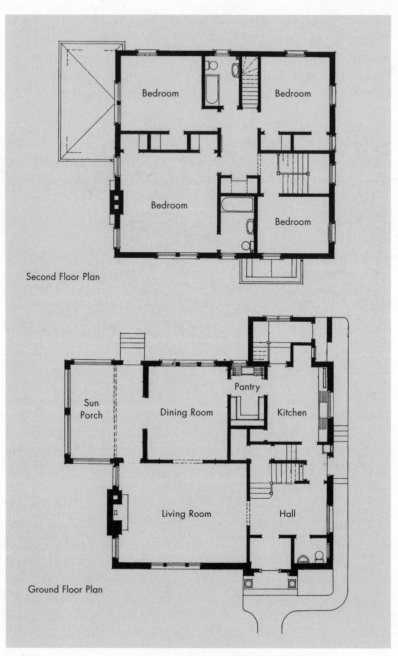

Bedroom

Bedroom

Bedroom

Bedroom

Second Floor Plan

Sun Porch

Dining Room

Pantry

Kitchen

Living Room

Hall

Ground Floor Plan

21. Residence, Albert Street, Kingston, 1922. The third floor is not shown.

Yet home buyers' tastes remained cautious, and interior layouts were slow to change. The traditional closed plan of smaller separate rooms persisted well into the century, even in buildings where space was at a premium. The plan for a bungalow farmhouse publicized by the government of British Columbia in 1916 called for a single-storey, 864 square foot (80 square metre) dwelling that included five rooms – 'will accommodate a family of four or five persons' the promotional literature advised (Figure 22). The early twentieth-century open plan continued to segregate the kitchen, though the remaining public rooms were often linked. A small two-bedroom bungalow designed by a leading Kingston architect shortly after the Second World War, when building materials were expensive and in short supply, also separated the living room from the combined kitchen and dining space, and this almost half a century after open planning had redefined home interiors (Figure 23). The same solution to the problem of interior design has persisted into the recent past, as we see in the simple layout of a government-funded two-storey row house rental complex built in Saskatoon in 1968 (Figure 24).

Often this conservative impulse was stronger still in the gracious homes of the wealthy. In its time the M.G. Angus residence in Westmount, Quebec, a flat-roofed international-style house designed in 1950, represented a daring stylistic innovation in one of Canada's most prestigious neighbourhoods. Yet it preserved the same separation of spatial functions we saw in the homes of the rich more than a century before, though of course some of the functions had changed dramatically by then (Figure 25).

Still the postwar era saw the triumph of flexibility and informality, at least in the middle-class home. The study transformed itself into the den, the kitchen sprouted a breakfast nook, and the living room abandoned most vestiges of its formal past as the parlour. The most important innovations, however, were new spaces for informal household and social life: the family and recreation rooms. Although the terms were used interchangeably, the latter was really the former's poor cousin. The tendency was to place the family room in an inviting space on the main floor, close to the kitchen, while consigning the recreation room to the basement. More recently still, suburban house design has reunited the kitchen and the family room, joining again what formality had once put asunder and restoring the home's ancient centre of sociability in the process.

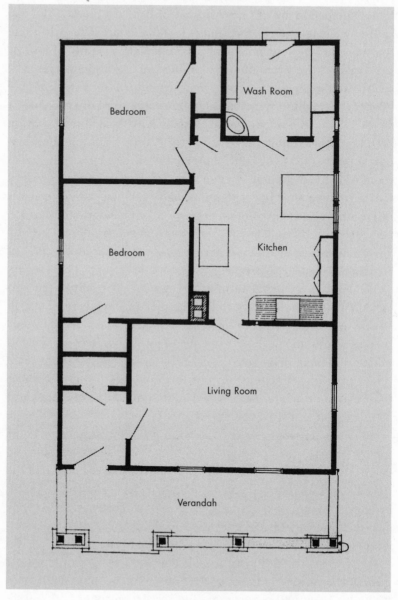

22. BC government plan for a bungalow farmhouse, 1916.

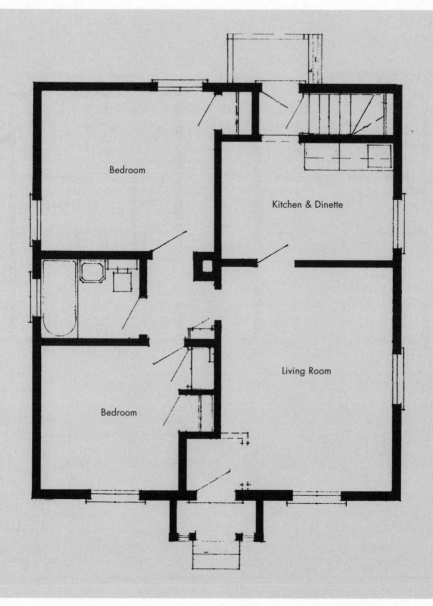

Bedroom

Kitchen & Dinette

Living Room

Bedroom

23. Detail of bungalow plan, Kingston, Ontario, or area, 1946.

Kitchen   Dining

Vest.

Living Room

Ground Floor Plan

Bedroom   Bedroom

Bathroom.

Bedroom   Bedroom

Second Floor Plan

24. Detail of plan for row housing,
Saskatoon, 1968.

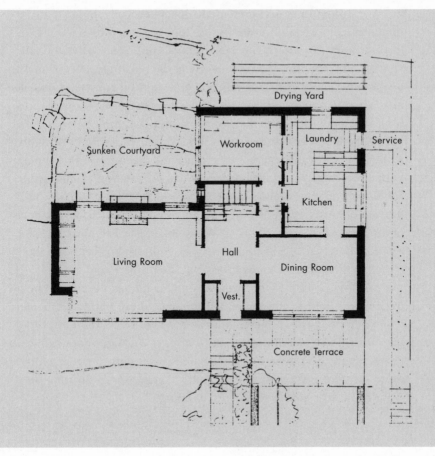

25. M.G. Angus residence, Westmount, Quebec, 1950.

An authentic expression of the postwar baby boom and its heightened sense of domesticity, the family room was intended for leisure, a space where the generations could come together for shared amusements: games, music, and, increasingly, television. In keeping with less formal fashions of entertaining guests at home, it also became a prime site of adult social gatherings, when couples invited friends in for drinks, snacks, and a game of cards – or, increasingly, an evening of television. An age of rising informality shifted the parlour's recreations to a new space more in keeping with newer, more relaxed forms of social relations. The family room was an important selling feature of upmarket houses built during the 1950s and '60s. The one illustrated in Figure 26, a model home built in 1962 in suburban White Rock, BC, is typical in every respect, down to the astonishingly uncomfortable round wicker chairs, which defy all known forms of the human anatomy.

Meanwhile those who lived in smaller homes discovered new frontiers in their undeveloped basements, where handy husbands could deploy urban pioneer skills and install a 'rec' room. In time, fake Western bars and English pubs graced the lower floors of tens of thousands of homes across Canada – a bit damp, rather chilly, dimly lit, and furnished with castoffs from upstairs. In time they usually became store rooms with a theme.

26. Demonstration home in White Rock, British Columbia, 1962.

Domestic Technology and Interior Spaces

During the French regime Canadiens commonly heated their homes with fireplaces and brick ovens, easy to make or inexpensive to acquire and thus widely used. But they also were inefficient. The better alternative was the cast iron stove, imported as a costly luxury or manufactured by the colonial iron industry at Saint-Maurice, which produced them in very small numbers in the years leading up to the Conquest. From the early nineteenth century, colonists generally adopted the iron stove or heater, except in places such as Lunenburg, where residents preferred the ceramic close stove of their German ancestors. Larger homes usually had two or three heaters, and rooms lacking them often were warmed by pipes running from stoves elsewhere in the house. A Canadian winter could be cruelly cold for the poor but, from what we can now tell, early-nineteenth-century Canadian homes generally were warm; in fact, English travellers sometimes complained of their oppressive heat. Iron stoves and heaters remained by far the most common devices for heating urban homes until well into the twentieth century. In rural places they were universal. As an old man, my grandfather Alex Hanley told me about his family's farm home near Baltic's Corners in Glengarry County, Ontario, during the 1890s. 'There were two wood-burning heaters in the house,' he recalled. In addition, 'the stove in the kitchen provided the heat there and that is where we lived most of the time.'[28]

The first effective domestic central heating system anywhere in North America seems to have been introduced in Quebec City in 1818.[29] But the technology was primitive and expensive, and so spread in a rather leisurely way during the rest of the century. From the 1850s wealthy Canadians adopted it in their homes but it remained a luxury for the favoured few until late in the century. Then, as technical improvements occurred and costs began to decline, it gradually became a fixture in the middle-class urban dwelling and in time trickled down to the working-class suburbs, the small towns, and the farmsteads of the nation. But progress remained slow. A 1937 survey of older Montreal working-class housing discovered that almost all of the 4,200 dwellings examined were warmed only by a cookstove. Still, conditions varied from one city to the next, even among those on the lower social margins. A similar study in Toronto three years earlier had found that, of the 5,060 working men's homes inspected, over 40 percent knew the joys of central heat. In fact, furnaces only overtook stoves and space heaters as the leading source of Canadian home heating during the 1950s, and it took another three decades before central heating became the birthright of us all. Rural dwellers and the poor were the last admitted to the charmed circle of automated warmth, in this way (as in so many others) living in conditions much like those their ancestors had known several generations earlier.[30]

The evolution of domestic lighting is quite a different story. Until well into the nineteenth century most Canadians lit their homes with candles and oil lamps. But these were expensive and smoky and they yielded a poor light. The kerosene lamp, introduced and refined during the early and middle years of the century, gradually supplanted candlelight with better and cheaper illumination. Juliana Ewing, a young British military officer's wife stationed in Fredericton during the late 1860s, observed that kerosene was in general use there because it provided good light and it cost less than candles. Then, in the dying years of the century, electric lights began to replace the kerosene lamp in turn, and over the coming decades the incandescent light bulb carved out the empire it rules today. It was cleaner, safer, more convenient, and (perhaps most important of all) very much cheaper than any other form of lighting. A recent estimate suggests that the cost of illumination has dropped by more than 99 percent over the past two centuries, the decline at its steepest during the late nineteenth and early twentieth centuries – when the electric light bulb conquered the open flame.[31]

Like many other domestic technological innovations, electric lighting first entered the homes of urban elites. But unlike the case of central heating, it quickly extended its reach into all but the poorest city houses, then moved rather more gradually into small town and rural dwellings. The survey of older Montreal working-class housing just mentioned noted that virtually all homes had electric lighting in 1937. The Toronto enquiry also found it in over 90 percent of the city's poorest homes.[32] In 1941 (the first year this information was gathered), some 70 percent of all Canadian homes boasted electric lighting. By then it was almost universal in cities and towns, and widely diffused in villages as well. Only farm dwellers lagged well behind the trend because electrification schemes were slow to penetrate rural Canada's dispersed settlements.[33] By 1959 the Dick family could enjoy its bounty even on the Arctic frontier (Figure 4). The incandescent light bulb, it seems, has been one of modernity's most egalitarian goods.

These improvements in heating and lighting had important effects on domestic social relations, access to personal space in particular. Normally household members could only use rooms that were warm and well lighted, at least during the cold dark months of the year. A large house with several ill heated or poorly lit rooms was functionally no bigger than a small one, for family members had to cluster together to share basic comforts. Even when homes had heaters in several rooms, the cost and trouble of keeping all of them lit at once encouraged family members to gather around a single source of warmth. Kerosene lamps had the same effect. They required careful tending; filling, cleaning, and wick trimming were time-consuming tasks that were much too dangerous to assign to the young. Nor was it safe to leave children alone with burning lamps. The chores and risks that lamps involved thus limited the number lit at any one time. Because the kitchen was often the warmest, best-lit room in the house it became the centre of family life, as my grandfather recollected. In his childhood reminiscences of winter evenings in late-nineteenth-century rural Quebec, author Robert Laroque recalled sitting with his parents in a single pool of lamplight close to a big stove, while his father read, his mother sewed, and all three of them drowsed in the heat.[34] Meanwhile his brothers and sisters did their schoolwork in a special room upstairs, supervised by a servant.

The interior photograph of John Beam's ranch house, some distance north of Cochrane, Alberta, during the 1890s, is a fine illustration of the powerful effect of a central light source on the social life of the home (Figure 27). Here two kerosene lamps bring the household together for a sociable evening of cards, conversation, and sewing. The eight people in the photograph are clustered together in a single small room, their attention focused by the shared pool of light. In this way older heating and lighting technologies restricted the use of space in the home, drawing household members into each other's company in the process.

27. Interior of John Beam's ranch house,
north of Cochrane, Alberta, c. 1890.

Central heating and the electric light altered these patterns dramatically. They were convenient, safe, and reliable, and they distributed domestic comforts throughout the home, making all rooms accessible to all family members at all times of the day in all seasons of the year. The electric lamp even offered the prospect of more than one light source in a single room. The result was that family members need no longer huddle together during the long cold evenings of a winter's night. They could retreat to the greater privacy of a separate focus of heat and light, or to the still greater privacy of another warm, well-lit room. These changes occurred at a point when the number of people in the household was shrinking and the physical size of the house was growing. The combination gave more and more Canadians opportunities to be alone within their own homes. By the mid-twentieth century many still lacked a room of their own, but most could lay greater personal claim to private places and spaces in their dwellings than all but their most privileged ancestors.

One thoughtful observer speculates that the modern generation gap might even be a product of the electric light.[35] He suggests that when the large families of yore gathered for an evening of school work, games, reading, needlecraft, and idle conversation, the older children's need for quiet led them to discipline their younger brothers and sisters, leaving their parents to act as mere referees. But once the revolution in lighting dispersed children throughout the home, the sibling wars dwindled to skirmishes and children abandoned the role of family policing to their parents. According to the hypothesis, the gap between the generations yawned at that point. We should always be cautious when faced with reductive arguments, and this one is an obvious tongue-in-cheek suggestion. But the larger point – that changes in domestic technology left a powerful imprint on family relations – is beyond question.

The Bathroom

From the standpoint of household privacy, however, the most dramatic technological change by far was the diffusion of the flush toilet. Unlike in British and European urban dwellings, where the indoor 'earth closet' was common long before the domestic sanitary revolution, the outdoor privy remained a near-universal feature of the Canadian home until the late nineteenth century. Indoors the chamber pot and the commode or *chaise percée* were in daily use, dumped regularly in the small house at the back of the lot.[36] When full, privies were commonly dug out and emptied into nearby fields, woods, water courses, vacant lots, or even city streets. The processes of meeting bodily needs were neither carefully hidden nor artfully disguised, and the odour of human wastes blended into the rich bouquet of everyday life indoors and outdoors alike. The triumph of the toilet was to change all this.

The toilet has a long and complex North American history. In the United States the first household plumbing fixtures began to appear during the mid-nineteenth-century decades, predating public water and sewer systems by at least a generation.[37] Householders improvised their own supplies by piping water from creeks and rivers or drawing it from cisterns and wells. They then discharged their wastes into private cesspools. Similar arrangements were probably made in Canada at this time, though they must have been quite uncommon for we no longer know anything about them.

The technology of the flush toilet had been under development since the late eighteenth century. The washdown model we're familiar with today, however, is based on a series of British innovations devised during the 1870s and 1880s.[38] Its broad diffusion depended heavily, as well, on access to running water supplies and sewer systems, costly services that appeared only gradually in nineteenth-century urban Canada. Two cities in the vanguard were Toronto and Saint John, which laid the first urban sewers in Canada during the 1830s. Yet development remained slow until the later years of the century. In 1874, only 15 percent of Toronto households had connections to the city's water system. From that point on, though, the rate of water and sewer line construction increased dramatically, in tandem with the rapid urban growth of the era. Only nine years later, 98 percent of Toronto dwellings were served by piped water. The situation in Montreal was broadly similar. On the eve of the First World War most Canadian cities and large towns could claim that water and sewer systems served the great majority of their households. In fact, by 1914 the sanitary revolution in the Canadian city had largely run its course.[39]

While the flush toilet had appeared in a few Canadian homes

by the early 1850s it remained a luxury enjoyed by the wealthy until late in the century. In the early 1880s architects could still design large Toronto upper-middle-class homes without providing for either a toilet or bathroom.[40] Then, when a superior technology and a watery infrastructure were finally in place, the outdoor privy began its dignified march from the back of the lot to a small room inside the home. Once commenced, its progress was steady if unspectacular.

Toronto's first comprehensive house-to-house public health inspection, conducted in 1885, revealed that 60 percent of all dwellings were still served by privies – half of them either full or foul. In 1911, when the city's sewer and water systems were well in place, almost half of the homes in its notorious central slum still relied on the outhouse, though indoor plumbing was more or less universal through the rest of the city. Public health advocates and reform-minded city councils continued to fight manfully against the privy, and within two decades it was a thing of the past throughout most of urban Canada. Every working-class Montreal dwelling inspected had an indoor toilet by the end of the 1930s, though a small proportion were shared by more than one household. Things were not quite so advanced in the poorer districts of Toronto, where only 87 percent of surveyed homes could boast such fixtures in the mid-1930s. Western Canadian cities enjoyed much the same conditions, though in some cases the Depression may have retarded development. In 1941, 29 percent of dwellings in Edmonton, for example, still lacked a flush toilet. But by this time it had become the very epitome of the modern domestic appliance – useful, clean, and efficient – a commonplace amenity in the urban Canadian household.[41]

Conditions in small towns, suburbs, and rural areas, in contrast, often lagged well behind. In 1941, only slightly more than half of all households in the nation had an indoor flush toilet, in many cases shared, while the outhouse continued to serve the needs of almost all others – a measure of how non-urban Canada remained at the time. The privy didn't disappear below the census takers' horizon until 1971, when the number of households still using one was too negligible to report.[42] By then, the great white porcelain fixture had become the item of choice in almost all Canadian homes, save the few still without running water or the even fewer owned by those ecologically minded souls who lived in harmony with nature and composted their own wastes.

The defeat of the privy has most often been viewed from the standpoint of public health and hygiene: the victory of enlightened social policy over ignorance and disease. But we've yet to pay much attention to its influence on one's sense of self and on social relationships. From the perspective of the individual, in particular, the larger significance of the sanitary revolution lies in the new meanings it imparted to human excretion. As the Swiss sociologist Norbert Elias long ago observed, from the Middle Ages an advancing sense of delicacy marked the long evolution of Western attitudes toward the body's excretory functions. Acts that once seemed natural gradually became encrusted with repugnance and shame, set apart from the public world by unconscious social command.[43] Over time this same process unfolded in Canada.

The domestication of defecation ended the age old outdoor exile of everyday body functions. It privatized elimination by confining it to an isolated space inside the home. Thereafter passing wastes became a more deeply personal matter, set well apart from the surrounding social world. Commodes and chamber pots remained, but over time their use was confined to the very young, the elderly, and the infirm – those considered less able and autonomous. In urban places elimination outside the home became a social and civic offence, especially in middle-class eyes. When faced with resistance to the new hygienic order, city fathers built public toilets and enforced their use through local by-laws.[44] But even these facilities concealed the processes of urination and defecation from public exposure by providing individual compartments for users.

As elimination became confined to a small indoor chamber a new and more powerful sense of shame attached itself to these normal body functions, as well as to the rooms where they were performed. A growing aversion to the odours of excreta accompanied the toilet on its journey into the home. The results were heightened embarrassment about passing body wastes and increasing sensitivity about giving offence while performing such acts. The need to eliminate these odours from the house became a particular concern.

These developments formed part of a broader international revolution in attitudes toward strong odours, a transformation explored by the French cultural historian Alain Corbin. According to Corbin, a new antipathy to unpleasant smells emerged among the French bourgeoisie during the nineteenth century, especially a growing revulsion toward body odours given off by strangers, but even toward those of family members as well.[45] Bourgeois opinion came to regard the stench of human wastes, in particular, as not just unpleasant but dangerous, a source of serious diseases and thus a threat to good health. The former tolerance for these odours declined as middle-class advocates condemned the lower orders for their offensive smells and tried to eliminate unpleasant odours within their own social ranks as well.

We see signs of this same unease in Canadian cities as the nineteenth century progressed. The odour of human excrement – what our Victorian ancestors euphemistically called 'night soil' – was a particular concern. Public health advocates repeatedly complained of the offensive smells that besieged their communities seasonally. During the summer heat, one Montreal reformer claimed in 1867, many householders opened their windows 'over the reeking fumes of the back courts [where privies were located], *because they could not bear the greater stenches of the street.*'[46] Civic officials condemned the outhouse as much for its smell as for its threat to public health, and they worked systematically to abolish it. Throughout the later nineteenth century, in response to public complaints, city councils in Montreal and Toronto and many other communities also tried to suppress noxious odours on the street, passing by-laws that enforced the odourless removal of garbage and human or animal wastes.[47]

Some indications suggest that a considerable personal reserve surrounded elimination habits long before the privy moved indoors. Separate outhouses for women and men were not uncommon, those for the former placed closer to the house. The new aversion to stenches, however, produced an acute sense of privacy about excretory habits, clearly reflected in the location of toilets inside the dwelling. In the mid-nineteenth-century homes of the wealthy, where the first toilets were installed, they often were placed in a room of their own approached through an anteroom. The G.W. Allen mansion is an example (Figure 13). Here two doors and a small empty chamber set the act and the actor apart from the rest of the household.[48]

Even in smaller dwellings, where space was at a premium, home designers took pains to install the toilet well away from the principal rooms. One common practice was to position it at the rear of the second storey, sharing as few common walls with other rooms as possible. In larger homes it could also be put next to the servants' room, where the problem of giving offence clearly didn't much matter (Figure 16). The small homes built in increasing numbers after the turn of the century presented a special design challenge. The floor plan in Figure 23, a cramped four-room bungalow of just over 600 square feet (55 square metres) built in the late 1940s, placed the tiny bathroom between the two bedrooms but separated it from the other rooms by a short corridor entered from the living room. When toilets were installed in older buildings, however, it wasn't always possible to take the same account of the need for their seclusion. As a result they might be put in less desirable locations (Figure 19, 2-6).

The convenience of a second toilet sometimes blessed more expensive homes even in the nineteenth century. At first they were often placed in a remote corner of the cellar, an indoor version of separate outhouses for men and women, for the cellar was to some extent a man's domain. Another solution, common in large two-storey Ontario homes built between the two world wars, was to place a toilet and wash basin in a small room beside the front entrance of the house, accessible to and yet apart from the public rooms on the main floor (Figure 21), a convention that continues in many suburban houses today. But the full flowering of domestic plumbing didn't reach the Canadian middle-class home until the 1960s, when the 'en suite' bathroom made its appearance in the better mass-produced suburban houses and apartment buildings. Previously found only in much more expensive houses, as Figure 21 again shows us, the en suite was a full bathroom attached to the main bedroom of the home. Its diffusion marked a further step in the subdivision of space within the home. Now the master and mistress of the house need no longer share their toilet and bath with other household members, claiming the still greater privacy of a bathroom of their own.

Which brings us to bathing. The history of the clean body has still to be written, important though the topic is. So what we know about our forbears' hygienic habits is based more on impressions than on evidence. A trip to an antique shop today shows us some of the equipment: the ubiquitous wooden washstands with their ceramic jugs and basins, and the occasional odd-shaped metal tub once placed before the kitchen stove for the Saturday night bath. Yet we know almost nothing about how often, and how thoroughly, Canadians washed themselves before the twentieth century. John Kenneth Galbraith's amusing tale of the turn-of-the-century Ontario farmer who thought he'd lost his vest on his annual bathing trip to Lake Erie, only to find it beneath his undershirt when he returned a year later, might seem the apocryphal tale of a good story teller. But with an octogenarian's clarity my grandfather recalled similar habits from the same period. In 1900, at the age of fifteen, he went to work for a merchant named Cameron in Dominionville, Glengarry County. 'Facilities such as we know them today were unknown at that time,' he told me toward the end of his life. 'You had a bath maybe once in six months. We must have smelled to high heaven although I never noticed it. Cameron didn't have a bathroom in his home.'[49]

It seems clear that very few Canadians had access to bathing facilities before the twentieth century, a situation they shared with most of the Western world. In France, for example, the custom of taking hot baths only developed during the early nineteenth century, and only among the bourgeoisie. Even then it remained a feminine luxury, indulged just once a month. Men used public baths if they bathed at all. The historian of water Jean-Pierre Goubert tells us that, in 1880, five out of six Americans had nothing more than a bucket and sponge to bathe with. It seems reasonable to believe that their northern neighbours fared no better, if as well.[50]

Occasionally Canada's civic leaders tried to improve the situation. In the 1860s, under pressure from the Montreal Sanitary Association, the city government opened two open-air floating summer public baths on the St Lawrence River. Intended for the urban working class, the first was built in the French-speaking east, the second in the English-speaking west.[51] Others followed over the next half century, though none was covered until the 1890s and none heated until the last years before the war. Winter cleanliness in Montreal must have remained a middle-class privilege.

In our terms public baths were swimming pools, but their promoters justified them on hygienic rather than recreational grounds. One Montreal community leader became particularly concerned for the needs of women because mixed-sex bathing was forbidden at the baths and women were only admitted during restricted hours. He observed that 'in almost every respectable poor person's house, two essentials necessary for health and comfort are entirely wanting, viz. baths and privacy. This great want would be largely supplied by public baths, an essential to health and godliness not only for mothers, but their daughters also.'[52] It's hard not to see bourgeois anxieties about working-class odours lurking beneath these campaigns.

But as for statistics we have few at hand. The Montreal and Toronto working-class housing surveys tell us that during the Depression, over 60 percent of homes in the Toronto sample had a bath though only 30 percent in the Montreal study were supplied with one. The Toronto figures, at least, compare favourably with the first national information available for 1941, which reveals that just under half of all Canadian homes then included a bath or shower, the proportion rising to more than 90 percent over the next three decades. By the '90s the bath or shower had become a near universal feature in Canadian homes, while over 30 percent included two or more bathrooms.[53]

Thus the Canadian bathroom is largely a twentieth-century development. In the small number of commodious nineteenth-century homes where plumbing was first installed, the toilet and bath were often placed in separate rooms. But the wall between them soon disappeared as the space set aside for these functions shrank, victim to economies in construction costs and a wish for larger rooms elsewhere in the house. Almost invariably the bathroom was little bigger than a good-sized closet, even in spacious and elegant homes, a cramped and concealed space set aside for intimate acts. Figure 28, an Edmonton bathroom in 1914, is characteristic.

From the outset three appliances formed the universal bathroom trinity: toilet, tub, and basin. Such refinements as showers only gradually claimed space, more often than not in the home's second

28. Bathroom, Edmonton, 1914.

bathroom, and for the most part during the last half-century, when the number of additional plumbing fixtures in middle-class homes has multiplied dramatically. The bidet, common in some European countries, has only recently arrived in the bourgeois Canadian bathroom, a fashionable testament to worldliness, travel, and hygienic refinement as much as to daily cleansing rituals.

The contemporary bathroom thus owes much of its utility to one of the great shifts shaping late-twentieth-century Western culture, our growing preoccupation with our own bodies and their odours, as well as the bodies of others. No longer just a space set apart for the unsocial acts of elimination and washing, the bathroom has become a private space to cleanse the body for personal pleasure and social presentation. Here the sensuous gratifications of grooming are combined with the elaborate and highly commercialized hygienic rituals of contemporary life, actions that have less to do with cleanliness itself than with preparation for social relations. In the privacy of the bathroom the body is now bathed, perfumed, and shaved, readied for its public role on the stage of daily life. The longstanding concern for offensive bathroom smells remains, but today it takes second place to the newer task of preparing the body for social display. Simple cleanliness is no longer enough; we now need to look and smell fresh and appealing as well.

The Parlour

Parlour, salon, sitting room, front room, living room. These were the labels most often attached to the room where the family met its visitors and presented its face to the outside world. In fact it's become a commonplace, if not a cliché, in writing the history of the house to describe the parlour as the home's most public space. But the Canadian experience has been rather more complex; experience has a way of confounding most simple categories, this one included. We'll see in due course that the kitchen has probably been the most accessible space in many Canadian homes, past and present alike. Still, the truth of the first proposition also can't be denied for, in most places and at most times, the front room probably has been the most public site in the dwelling.

Large Canadian residences have no doubt always had one or more rooms where guests could be entertained. But eighteenth-

and early-nineteenth-century small homes often lacked a parlour. During the first part of the nineteenth century, however, the front room began to establish itself in most dwellings across Canada and thereafter it proved remarkably enduring. From that point on until the age of the open plan, even very small homes designated one room as such. The salon made its appearance in modest rural French-Canadian houses at this time, while the houses that poor Irish settlers in Ontario and the Atlantic colonies built after the 'shanty' phase of frontier development usually had a front room as well. In fact, spaces set aside for special occasions were a feature of domestic arrangements in almost all communities, even when dwellings had very few rooms. The most common house form among Ukrainian settlers in early-twentieth-century Alberta was a simple two-room home, one a kitchen and living room used for all aspects of everyday life, the other intended only for formal events.[54]

Still, room designations are one thing, room uses quite another. How Canadians lived in their parlours isn't all that clear. The handsome drawing room in which the Woolseys posed was probably the artist's invention, a gracious setting intended to add further dignity to a flattering family portrait (Plate 1). Unfortunately, the genteel English artists who left us such a rich visual record of nineteenth-century Canadian life were much more interested in the natural than in the social world around them and so painted few indoor scenes. Later, when photography replaced painting as the main means of depicting reality, aesthetic principles and technical limitations guided early photographers away from mundane life and toward carefully composed representations of families, their homes, and possessions. These pictures had powerful symbolic value but on the surface, at least, they don't tell us much about domestic life in former times. We also have the written record – letters, diaries, reminiscences, travellers' accounts – which offer glimpses into the everyday experience. But as social historians know all too well, many things we now wish to know about the past were thought too ordinary or unimportant to warrant writing down. So we're left with bits and pieces when attempting to understand domestic spaces in earlier times.

One powerful myth about the nineteenth-century parlour is that it was a formal room, seldom used by the family save on special occasions. But living space in small homes was scarce enough that householders must often have used whatever room was available to their best advantage, parlours included. Catherine Ellice's mid-nineteenth-century sketch of the manor house drawing room on the Seigneurie at Beauharnois (Plate 2) is scarcely typical, but it reveals a place of comfortable informality, obviously used by the family on an everyday basis. We see another example in the courtship diary kept during the same period by the Quebec city clerk George Jones, which offers some revealing glimpses of the social life of his beloved, Honorine Tanswell, and her household.[55] The Tanswells were a prominent, monied family in the city, with strong connections through marriage to both the French- and the English-speaking communities. They entertained family and friends in their parlour at suppers, card games, and the like, often several times a week. When no guests were present they used the same room for various recreations. In many other cases, however, the parlour retained the air of a place set apart from everyday affairs.

No doubt practices varied widely, some families preserving their parlours for special occasions, others using them for daily activities. There may well have been a trend toward growing formality in the urban middle-class parlour as the Victorian era matured, but the evidence is far from conclusive. The parlour's clear identification as a formal place – so characteristic of middle- and working-class respectability in Victorian Britain – wasn't always all that obvious in Canada. Moreover, everyday social relations didn't place the same premium on formality and ceremony in the countryside as in the city, with the result that the rural parlour may well have been a more informal, family-centred place than its urban counterpart.[56]

As the home's most public room, the parlour played a powerful symbolic role in representing the family to its guests. Its furnishings and decorations spoke of their tastes and interests, as well as their claims for status in the unspoken hierarchies of community life. Like a museum exhibit under glass, it displayed the family to the outside world through its material possessions: its links with the past through family portraits, its wealth through its furnishings, its refinements through books, pictures, *objets d'art*, and musical instruments.

29. Salon of the Lowe family home, Ottawa, 1890.

Three contrasting examples illustrate the point clearly. Mr Lowe's elegant formal Ottawa salon, pictured in the 1890 photograph in Figure 29, is rich in the symbols of worldly success: handsome furniture, sculpted plaster work, brocaded window hangings, a square grand piano, and, most esoteric of all, a harp. Here stood forceful claims to the Lowes' social and cultural aspirations, a material harvest reaped through a lifetime of worldly success. The obvious intent here was to display and impress. (I have to admit my suspicions about the harp; in the jumped-up lumber town that Ottawa was, it was probably admired rather more often than played.)

Yet even those who lived in poverty could represent the self through an exhibition of modest possessions. The early-twentieth-century Toronto slum dwellers in Figure 7 hung a revealing collection of cheap reproductions on one wall of their single room.

Jean-François Millet's *The Angelus* and a palm branch testify to religious faith, while a horse's head and a pastoral scene suggest an interest in country life. The popular print of Edward VII reveals a commitment to the monarchy and the ideals of empire though, if we note the whisk and picture hanging over the portrait of Queen Victoria – who else would have had such famous plump forearms? – perhaps we shouldn't overestimate their patriotism. These pictures speak of a brave attempt to turn a shabby room into one with a personal face. They also hint at richer lives lived in the past and hopes for better things to come. They must have reminded the poor family in the photograph, as they do the viewers, that there was more to their lives than met the eye.

Some 4,000 kilometres west at about the same time, the Boose family were photographed in their farmhouse parlour near Vulcan, Alberta (Figure 30). They lived in a simple four-room settler's home surrounded by the few possessions they'd brought with them to the prairies. Family portraits hang between the studs on the still unfinished interior walls, the parents sit in two simple wicker chairs while daughter Edith is perched on the stool before the piano, the one prized piece of furniture in the photograph. Here we glimpse the lineage, the brave hopes, and the modest material achievements of a family that had chosen a fresh start in an untried location.

The piano occupied a particularly important place, both symbolic and practical, in the middle-class Canadian parlour. The modern pianoforte developed in western Europe during the late eighteenth and early nineteenth centuries and by the 1820s – when the first large-scale British migrations to Canada had begun – it had assumed its modern form.[57] Its construction technology spread quickly, and before long pianos were widely manufactured in Europe and North America, an early consumer commodity mass produced for a growing bourgeois market. By midcentury it had established itself as a mark of prosperity and cultural sophistication in middle-class homes everywhere in the Western world, Canada included, and it remained the most widely diffused household status symbol until well into the twentieth century. A piano in the front room set a family apart from the neighbours who lacked one; not only was it expensive but it displayed its owners' leisure and cultural refinement to friends and neighbours.

30. Parlour of the Boose family home, near Vulcan, Alberta, 1910.

The piano was pre-eminently a woman's instrument. Nineteenth-century notions of middle-class femininity highly valued musical ability and held skilled piano playing the supreme cultural accomplishment, along with a fine singing voice. But even indifferent capacity was valued as a sign of female gentility and cultivation. In an age when families made their own music women held a central place in home and community entertainment, very often as pianists. Young middle-class women often took special pains to develop their keyboard skills because prospective suitors commonly regarded a musical education as especially attractive in a wife. For this reason the piano could play an important part in a woman's courtship strategies, to say nothing of those of parents anxious to advance their daughters' marital interests. Thus for well over a century the piano held a central place in the middle-class Canadian parlour. In 1828, for instance, it took up much of the small sitting room that the English immigrant Southby Gapper built for his mother and sister in the attic of his pioneer Upper Canadian home.[58] Some three generations later the delightfully pompous photograph of Mr and Mrs Hutchinson at home, taken in Port Perry, Ontario, in 1900, illustrates the piano's role even more clearly

(Figure 31). The Hutchinsons themselves form part of the display, formally dressed and carefully placed in a tableau of their material and cultural attainments, their modest upright the centrepiece of their parlour, the musically accomplished wife an obvious ornament in the home.

The fireplace, or hearth –*foyer en français* –played an even more powerfully symbolic role in the Canadian dwelling, one that persists to the present day. From time immemorial until the late eighteenth century, of course, the fireplace had served highly practical as well as symbolic ends throughout Europe and America. The source of the home's winter heat and much of its light, it was also the place where most food was cooked. But as more efficient iron stoves replaced less efficient fireplaces, the latter lost most of their usefulness. If anything the fireplace became something of a problem. It took up valuable indoor space and, unless its chimney were blocked, allowed heat to escape up the flue. One common remedy in older buildings was to combine the two technologies by fitting new stoves into old fireplaces, venting the smoke up existing chimneys.

Yet the fireplace persisted in the Canadian home long after it could claim much utility. The G.W. Allen house in Toronto, an early example of a centrally heated dwelling, had at least four fireplaces in its main floor public rooms, with an additional four in upstairs bedrooms and dressing rooms (Figures 12 and 13). The cramped, turn-of-the-century Toronto worker's row house in Figure 18, also centrally heated, included a parlour fireplace as well. Early apartment designers, owners, and renters felt the need for a hearth strongly enough that gas fireplaces were incorporated into some of the more luxurious buildings constructed early in the century. Plans for the very small two-bedroom post-Second World War bungalow in Figure 23 even made provision for an electric fireplace. These devices made small contributions to home heating but by no means enough to justify their installation.

So we need to look elsewhere to explain the enduring presence of the fireplace in the Canadian parlour. Certainly no one can deny the appeal of a crackling fire on a stormy winter's eve. But these charms can't offer us a full explanation either. Instead we need to recognize the age old symbolic power of the fireplace as the centre of warmth and nurture within the home. The words 'hearth' and

31. Mr and Mrs Hutchinson at home, Port Perry, Ontario, c. 1900.

'foyer,' in fact, have long been synonyms for 'household,' and the fireplace the metaphorical focal point of family life. Indeed, the symbolic meaning of the hearth – the one place in the dwelling where family members have always gathered for warmth, nourishment, and mutuality – is just as significant as its practical value in explaining its continued appeal.

Consider for a moment *Au foyer domestique*, an engraving by E.J. Massicotte published in 1900. Here we see an idealized scene of French-Canadian bourgeois domesticity, the couple seated before the hearth while they share (somewhat unequally to be sure) the quiet pleasures of the evening newspaper (Figure 32). It doesn't really matter that the fire seems not to be lit. The important fact is the central place of the *foyer* in this vision of Québécois domestic life, a site as much symbolic as real.

In Figure 33 we pass from the ideal to the real, or at least a carefully composed version of idealized reality. In fact, the family at home in the parlour was a common genre in high Victorian photography, the equivalent of the Woolsey family portrait from early in the century. This photograph of an apparently middle-class Toronto family around 1900 is typical. Mom and dad sit in front of the fireplace surrounded by the trophies of their worldly success, he with book in hand and she with smile on face, their older children playing happily on the floor, their youngest lovingly enfolded in its mother's arms. The only incongruous note here is the faraway look in father's eyes. Here, too, the hearth provides the setting for this happy family scene.

As symbol and physical object, the hearth and the piano reached the peak of their domestic influence during the first half of the twentieth century. Since then the piano, in particular, has been in steady decline. In the '60s the guitar – far less costly, a great deal easier to play, and much more egalitarian – replaced it as the instrument of choice in the average family household. At the same time the piano lost its dominant position in the world of commercial music. Mass broadcasting, sound systems, and recordings have spread the voice of popular music into the darkest corners of the Canadian home, devaluing musical skills in the process. The piano certainly retains a presence in many middle-class dwellings, but it now performs much more limited musical and social functions.

32. E.J. Massicotte, *Au foyer domestique*, 1900.

33. Unidentified adults and children, Toronto, c. 1890-1900.

34. Canadian living room, 1956.

Increasingly it's been confined to the classical and jazz repertoires – and thus to the more able, ambitious students, those who wish to master these difficult genres. The power of the piano as a status symbol remains, though limited to the grand, not the upright.

As for the hearth in the parlour, it persists to this day in wood, coal, gas, and electric forms. But it's become rather less common than it once was. It remains a fixture in the homes of the wealthy, and in those of the suburban middle class (Figures 25 and 26). Sometimes it can even be found in the luxury apartment. But it's long since fallen victim to building cost efficiencies in the smaller houses and apartments produced for middle- and low-income consumers (Figures 24, and 48 to 52).

Not only that but the twentieth century has brought unprecedented challenges to the fireplace as a focus of family life. First radio and then – much more dramatically – television shifted domestic sociability away from hearthside family amusements toward more passive forms of shared entertainment. Nor should we forget how sudden the TV invasion was. In 1953, when the first national statistics were gathered, 10 percent of Canadian homes had a set. By the end of the decade, a mere seven years later, the proportion approached 80 percent.[59] Once introduced, the TV quickly became the focal point of any room in which it was located. It certainly enjoys pride of place in the 1956 National Film Board photograph 'Modern Canadian Living Room,' which portrays with obvious approval the spare furnishings and uncluttered decor of a postwar urban middle-class living room (Figure 34). Here the fireplace and the piano seem banished from the modern home. Even symbolic meaning of the hearth has slowly atrophied. We now stand generations away from the world displayed by our pioneer museums, when the fact and the metaphor of the hearth were one. It's now increasingly hard to view the living-room fireplace as anything more than a place to light a cheery little blaze when friends come by for dinner or, in the realtor's language, a 'feature' that raises a home's resale value.

The Kitchen

In a world of shifting descriptions of rooms and their uses, the kitchen has long been a fixed point on the compass. It's always been the place in the home where food is prepared. It has served many other purposes too, but its core function has remained constant. In the one-room dwelling the kitchen was little more than the corner set aside for cooking. In homes with more than a single room, almost invariably one has been identified as the kitchen, though we do find a few exceptions. Still, it seems almost safe to claim that a house without a kitchen isn't really a home.

Kitchens have varied dramatically in size, shape, and function over the long history of the Canadian house. Studies of the traditional French-Canadian home don't identify a *cuisine* until the end of the eighteenth century. They refer instead to a *salle commune,* the central space in the home where most daily activities unfolded – cooking included – even when the house had several rooms.[60] This room was usually large, often the largest in the dwelling. By the beginning of the nineteenth century a somewhat smaller kitchen, perhaps with a narrower range of functions, began to emerge in rural houses, as well as a summer kitchen located in an annex. It also seems that some of the social functions of the *salle commune* were then being lost to the salon, a room just making its appearance in the rural Quebec dwelling at that time.

We know rather less about the home's interior in early English Canada. The careful investigation of older French-Canadian dwellings hasn't been entirely duplicated in the rest of the country. But what we do know suggests that the kitchen in the small English-Canadian colonial house passed through much the same evolution, though over a shorter time span. During the first half of the nineteenth century, for instance, Irish settlers in Ontario and New Brunswick built rural homes whose kitchens took up more than half the floor space.[61] It was the place where family members spent most of their time indoors and where neighbours visited when they dropped by.

In some parts of Canada the country kitchen still clings to its role as the family and social centre of the house. The folklorist Gerald Pocius has recently explored domestic spaces in the Newfoundland outport village of Calvert; his notes are relevant here.[62] According to Pocius the Calvert kitchen remains the focus of most activity in the household today. In older homes, especially, it's dominated by a large wood stove, still the only source of heat in many village houses. There are chairs and a table, for all meals are taken here too. Most kitchens also include a day bed, where family members can take an afternoon nap or friends can sit when they come in for a chat. The home's other rooms are intended only for quite specific purposes, the bedrooms exclusively for sleeping and the front room largely for special occasions. The front entrance to the house is seldom used and almost everyone enters through the back door, which normally opens directly into the kitchen. Because Calvert is a small community where everyone knows everyone else, doors are seldom locked and friends never knock before entering. They simply open the door, walk in, and begin to converse. In most homes the normal day consists of a series of such comings and goings by family members and friends. Thus the Calvert kitchen is, in a very real sense, one of the most public spaces in town.

We might think Calvert an isolated example. After all, small places like this sometimes seem living museums of customs common in times long past. Nor can there be any doubt that such practices were once widespread. The family letters and diaries left us by our ancestors reveal many glimpses of them from the late eighteenth century onward. But we shouldn't think Newfoundland such a special case. On any drive along the back roads of the Canadian prairies today we can see a curious sight: farmhouses without front steps, which leaves their front doors suspended about a metre off the ground. Most of these homes were built in the '50s and '60s, based on designs then widely used in the swelling suburbs of nearby cities. The plans conformed to urban social practice, where the front door was the more formal and public entrance to the home. It led into a vestibule or hall and then to the living room, the most public place in the home, where the family met and entertained guests. But rural prairie social life, like that in Calvert, has long been more informal than this housing design suggests. It too has centred on the kitchen, entered directly from the back door. In fact, some prairie farmhouses lack front steps because their owners have had so little use for a formal entrance that they've never needed a front door. Here the kitchen remains what it has long been: the heart of home life.

The more limited-purpose kitchen seems to have appeared first in the grand houses of the early nineteenth century. That in Acacia Grove (Figure 11) was located in the basement, according to the upper-middle-class English custom, and so doesn't appear on the drawing. In other substantial houses the kitchen stood on the main floor, close to the dining room but as far from the other public rooms as possible; it was intended only for food preparation (Figure 35; see also Figure 12). As we see from the floor plans in Figures 15, 18, and 19, the amount of space set aside for a kitchen toward the end of the nineteenth century was largely a function of the size of the house. We shouldn't be surprised to discover that big homes had big kitchens and little homes little ones. But rather more important, the kitchen almost invariably stood apart from the rest of the dwelling, separated at least by a wall and usually by its location at the rear of the house. The open plan imported by the bungalow after 1900 didn't extend the principle of openness to kitchens. It merely reduced their size while preserving their exile at the back of the dwelling.[63] Even in early apartment blocks, where designers and builders often saved space by minimizing kitchen size, walls and doors still separated it from the rest of the suite, as we can see in the 1940s photograph of an early-twentieth-century Montreal apartment kitchen (Figure 36; see also Figures 44 and 45).

In time the barriers between cooking and dining began to crumble and the urban kitchen started to provide its own eating area. But this practice didn't become widespread until the 1950s, when formality in family dining customs also began to erode. Figure 37 illustrates the modern kitchen of the urban middle-class home of the '50s, replete with up-to-date electrical appliances, large built-in cupboards, extensive counter space and, in the foreground, the kitchen table and chairs, where mom, dad and the kids took breakfast, lunch, and supper. The dining room was now used only on special occasions. Yet here too the kitchen remained apart from the rest of the house.

The true open plan revolution in kitchen design occurred only in the 1960s. In apartments, particularly, the need for efficient use of floor space reduced the kitchen to a galley and opened it to the dining and living areas. In the early 1960s Winnipeg apartment plan shown in Figure 38 the kitchen formed part of a large open space intended for the many social activities of the household, cooking and eating included. Only the furnishings, we can assume, subdivided the room by function. The American architectural historian Elizabeth Cromley points out that this new 'living-dining-kitchen room,' found in both the middle-class house and the apartment of the period, rested on major changes to food preparation practices in the postwar North American home. Among the most important were technological advances such as better electric refrigerators and more reliable plumbing fixtures (which improved kitchen cleanliness and reduced offensive smells), the new availability of prepared foods from grocery shops, the disappearance of servants from all but the wealthiest households, and a popular redefinition of kitchen work as public, pleasurable, and sociable – to the point at which some men were willing to take up cooking themselves.[64] Together these changes redefined the place of the kitchen in the late-twentieth-century home. Absorbed once again into the spaces used for everyday family life, the kitchen had come full circle.

Finally, three concluding points about the social history of the Canadian kitchen. First, wherever and whenever the separation of

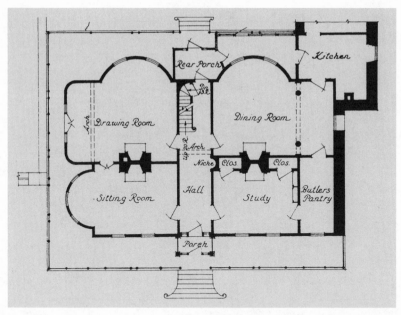

35. Gorsebrook, near Halifax, early nineteenth century, plan of ground floor.

36. Apartment kitchen, Montreal, c. 1947.

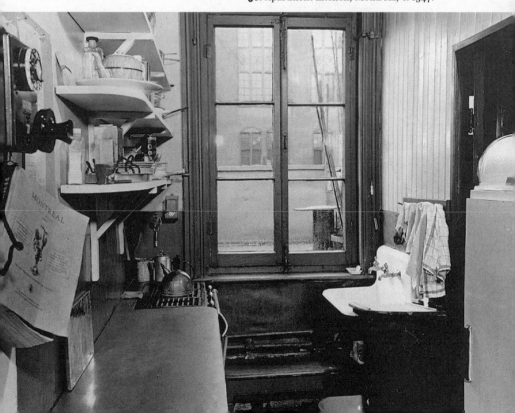

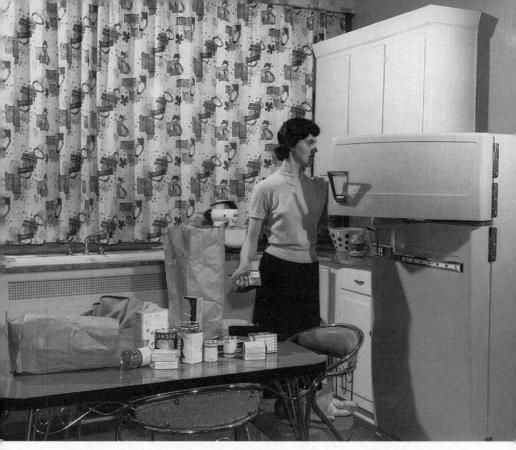

37. Canadian kitchen, 1956.

38. Floor plan of apartment, Winnipeg, 1961-2.

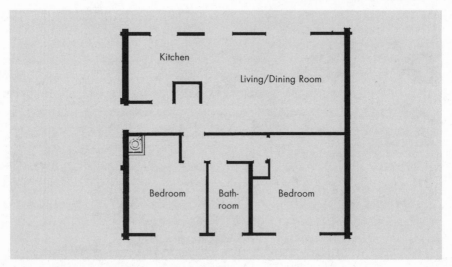

Kitchen

Living/Dining Room

Bedroom

Bath-
room

Bedroom

the kitchen from the rest of the house occurred it had an especially important impact on women. As long as family life centred on this room, women remained at its heart even as they worked. In fact, the kitchen was a woman's domain and the informal authority governing the kitchen was hers. But as it shrank and became a more specialized space, the focus of family life moved elsewhere in the home. This process tended to isolate the housewife from the rest of the household. In her thoroughly modern, turn-of-the-century Toronto kitchen Mrs Arthur Beales may well have been the monarch of all she surveyed, but where were her subjects (Figure 39)?

Second, in any discussion of housing innovation it's easy to lose sight of its absence, to forget that most people have lived domestic life far from the cutting edge of change. The wealthy and well-to-do have usually been first to enjoy the benefits of whatever improvements entered the home in the name of modernity. But in most cases the process of diffusion has been lengthy and the poor, in particular, often have long been denied living conditions that the privileged could take for granted. The contrast between the spacious electric kitchen of the '50s in Figure 37 and its cramped counterpart

39. Mrs Arthur Beales in her kitchen, Toronto, c. 1903-13.

in a Toronto Cabbagetown slum of the same period (with its wood-burning stove and inconvenient sink) has something to teach us about social inequalities in midcentury urban Canadian housing (Figure 40). That between suburban comfort and the rural poverty shown in Figure 41 – a 1966 kitchen in a run-down rural home near Drumheller, Alberta, which even lacked running water – is more striking still. The kitchen in this photograph has much more in common with those of the late nineteenth century than with its big-city show-home contemporaries. To live in poverty, so it seems, was to live in the past.

Third, we shouldn't be beguiled by the common fallacies that modern is better, progress is improvement, and backwardness is deprivation. Even a glance at the history of the kitchen indicates that domestic life has been a good deal more complex than slogans suggest. Figure 42 reveals a very simple kitchen in a very simple home – uncovered rafters on the ceiling, a few sticks of furniture scattered about, small cupboards covered by cloth hangings instead of doors, and pride of place to an old wood-burning stove. It might well be a pioneer homestead or the poor early-twentieth-century home of a family of limited means.

But we should spare our concern for its residents' welfare because this was a summer cottage: Cooking Lake, Alberta, 1945. In fundamentals it probably differed little from thousands of its kind, the summer homes many middle-class Canadians had built in growing numbers since the later nineteenth century. Often small, crudely built, and furnished with castoffs, cottages offered a retreat to older domestic ways. In fact, much of their appeal lay in the promise of a simpler life, bread from the wood-stove oven just like grandma baked it, families nestled before the fire on a stormy summer evening, friends gathered around a simple table heaped with food.

Like most common images of family life in earlier times, that of the summer cottage is shot through with myths. In fact, grandma had been only too pleased to get rid of the old stove because it was dirty, hot, and unreliable. But facts have done little to dim the bright charm of the idea itself, for the summer cottage has long exerted a powerful claim on the Canadian imagination. Year after year cottagers have happily passed their summers in crowded, ill-lit, and

40. A. Muir and Mrs Muir with their children in kitchen of an old house in Cabbagetown, a slum district in the east end, Toronto, 1949.

41. Substandard housing, Drumheller, Alberta, July 1966.

42. Kitchen of a summer home, Cooking Lake, Alberta, 1945.

badly furnished dwellings, using sanitary facilities gladly rejected by their grandparents, and eating food ill cooked on wood stoves that only a tiny minority know how to use, let alone do so safely. Of course, much of the appeal of the cottage has lain elsewhere, in the leisurely tempo of vacation life, in the lake or stream or mountain nearby. Still the fact remains that, given the option, for more than a century tens of thousands of Canadians have chosen to spend a significant part of each year living in what might otherwise be labelled substandard housing. What sets them apart from the chronically ill housed is the fact that they've had the choice.

The Bedroom

As with most other rooms we've discussed, the bedroom was largely an invention of the late eighteenth and early nineteenth centuries. Until then all but the most privileged colonists lived in one or two rooms, as we've seen, and beds stood throughout their homes. Some early French immigrants introduced the closed 'box bed' or *lit clos* of northwestern France to the new world. The American colonist Robert Hale described them after he visited a few Acadian houses in 1731: 'Their Bedrooms are made something after ye manner of a Sailor's Cabbin, but borded all round about the bigness of ye Bed, except one little hole on the Foreside, just big eno' to crawl into, before which is a Curtain drawn & a Step to get into it, there stands a Chest.' Wherever box beds existed they must have been the privilege of parents. But accounts of the early French-Canadian dwelling mention them so seldom that they were probably the exception rather than the rule.[65]

The absence of bedrooms persisted well into the nineteenth century in both French and British Canada, town and countryside alike. In the small homes of labouring people beds were placed wherever there was room. Children might sleep in an attic or loft but these could prove cold during the long nights of the bitter winter months. In many cases dividing the room with curtains was the only possible defence for marital intimacy. Sometimes country homes were more spacious than city ones and so offered more possibilities for separate sleeping arrangements. An early-nineteenth-century English traveller observed that rural houses generally had one or two beds in each room no matter how many chambers they included.

In winter, he noted, the man of the house often slept by the kitchen stove so he could tend the fire in the middle of the night.[66]

When houses were roomy enough to allow subdivision, interior spaces were allocated according to a subtle calculus based on age, sex, and power. Whenever possible the married couple asserted its priority and claimed a bedroom for itself – a retreat from the clamours of family life and a sanctuary for sexual intimacy. Old age also demanded its due and often received it by legal provision. Until the end of the nineteenth century wills customarily required heirs to provide a separate room for widows, along with a cash allowance and adequate amounts of food, fuel, and clothing.

On the other hand children and youths shared bedrooms, even beds, with same-sex brothers and sisters, a feature of family living arrangements throughout northwestern Europe and North America from time out of mind well into the twentieth century. The custom was universal in Canada as well, even among the wealthy, until reduced family size aligned the number of children in the family with the number of rooms and beds available in the home. During the early years of the nineteenth century the Woolseys' three boys slept in one room while their only daughter had another to herself. At about the same time Louisa Collins, an eighteen-year-old Nova Scotia farm girl and one of eight daughters in her family, shared a bed with her younger sister Phebe.[67]

Such arrangements were related to household size and wealth as much as to living space. In large families room sharing was almost always necessary, and poverty increased the likelihood that two or three children would sleep in a single bed. The oldest and youngest of each sex, however, might enjoy the luxury of sleeping alone for some of their childhood years, the former before their younger siblings were out of the crib, the latter after their elders had left home. An only daughter or son in a family with several children of the other sex might enjoy the special privilege of a private bedroom during adolescence, at least by the late nineteenth century, when the special needs of that phase of life came to be widely recognized. Very young children commonly shared their parents' beds, or so it seems from the number of infant deaths caused by 'overlaying' that cropped up in nineteenth-century coroners' inquests. Throughout the nineteenth century in much of the Western world, however, awareness grew of the need for the sexes and the generations to sleep in separate beds, if not rooms. Lurking behind this trend we glimpse fears of sexual impropriety and infanticide, and also of ill-defined 'family odours' condemned by the nineteenth-century olfactory revolution that I've already discussed. As for servants, they usually had a room each. The Woolseys always provided their female servants with a separate chamber, though in some of their homes the manservant had to sleep in the kitchen.[68]

By the twentieth century these conditions had begun to change except among the poorest of the poor. The single room depicted in Figure 7, home to one of Toronto's truly impoverished families, was probably partitioned by curtains at night as it was with laundry by day. But by the time this photograph was taken on the eve of the First World War, only a small and disadvantaged minority of urban Canadians lived this way. The survey of Montreal working-class housing conditions we've noted before found an average household size of 4.5 persons during the late 1930s (just over one person per room) and slightly less than one bed per inhabitant. Obviously the bedrooms in these homes were shared in the traditional manner, but by then there were enough beds to go round. Nevertheless, there were – and have always been – exceptions. Pocius mentions that family members might still sleep three and four to a bed in late-twentieth-century Calvert. But by the post-First World War era the vast majority of Canadians could look forward to their own bed at night. Most of those who shared would have done so by choice.[69]

I've already commented on the location of bedrooms and needn't cover that ground again here. Yet we also need to note the general trend from the eighteenth century on toward separating bedrooms from the rest of the house, at least in larger dwellings. The bedrooms in the eighteenth-century Paradis home shared connecting doors with one another, as well as with the adjacent salon and kitchen (Figure 9). Those in the large wooden house that the painter Antoine Plamondon built in 1846 at Pointe aux Trembles, Quebec, weren't linked with each other but still led off the salon – and perhaps the kitchen as well (Figure 43). In both dwellings a single wall divided sleeping space from the rest of the house, and residents passed directly from the public rooms into the bedrooms.

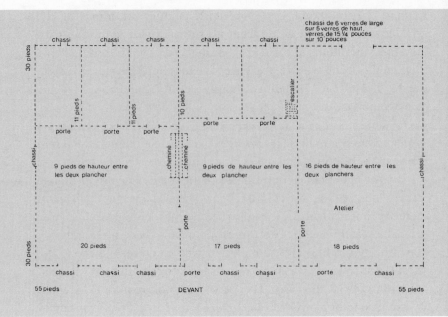

43. Plan for Antoine Plamondon's house, Pointe aux Trembles, Quebec, 1846.

But the nineteenth- and twentieth-century tendency was to seclude bedrooms further by isolating them from one another and by grouping them at a distance from other parts of the home. In many cases this meant locating the sleeping area upstairs, in others placing entrances to bedrooms in a hallway rather than a living or dining room (Figures 16 to 18). By the mid-twentieth century architects and builders were concealing family bedroom doors from visitors' eyes even in very small single-floor dwellings (Figure 23). The same principles guided apartment planning from the outset, though practice occasionally strayed from principle until the design problems raised by a new building form could be resolved. Compare the layout of units in the 1910 Toronto apartment block in Figure 44 with that of the Kingston complex in Figure 45, built two decades later. The Kingston apartment grouped bedrooms according to principle: at one end of the flat, separated from the living area by the kitchen and bathroom. In the earlier Toronto building no such rule guided the architect, who placed its bedrooms in a variety of ways.

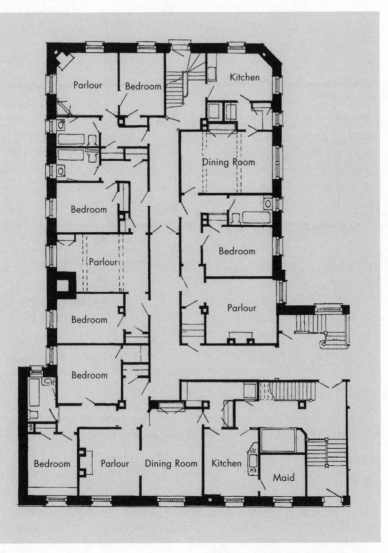

44. Detail of plan for eight-storey apartment building for the corner of Bloor and North streets, Toronto, 1910.

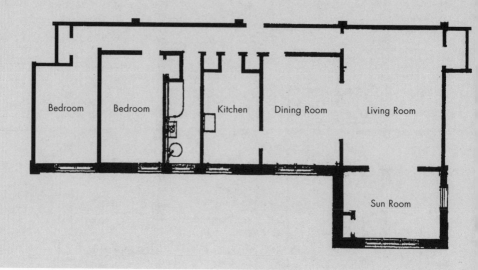

45. Detail of plan for a proposed apartment building at the intersection of Sydenham and William streets, Kingston, Ontario, 1928.

The important point to note is that, once set apart from the rest of the Canadian home, the bedroom was usually accessible only to family members. The old European aristocratic and bourgeois notion of the boudoir, a large room with sleeping and other furnishings where a woman might entertain visitors, had little if any currency in nineteenth-century Canada and certainly none in the twentieth. The splendid Victorian mansions of the nation's wealthiest families invariably included large, handsomely appointed bedrooms. But just as invariably they were located upstairs, well away from the home's public spaces. The rich entertained their guests in the drawing room, the dining room, or the library, not the far more intimate atmosphere of the bedroom (Figures 12 and 13). In more modest homes, sleeping spaces shrank to utilitarian size. The late Victorian middle-class bedroom might serve as a quiet retreat from the claims of family life, but it was seldom large enough to receive visitors even if custom had allowed it.

Plate 1
William Berczy
The Woolsey Family
Quebec City, 1809
(National Gallery of Canada
Ottawa, #5857)

Plate 2
Drawing room of the manor house
on the Seigneurie of Beauharnois,
Quebec, mid-nineteenth century

Plate 3
James Pattison Cockburn
Point Levis, 1829

Plate 4
Henry Martin
At Pinegrove, May 10, 1856

Plate 5
Anonymous
View of Guelph in 1831
The front door of the farmhouse in
the centre of the engraving faces the
river in the foreground, away from
the road that crosses the river.

Plate 6
(facing page, top)
Captain Dick's Cottage
c. 1830s

Plate 7
Looking south from the Citadel
Montreal, Lower Canada
early nineteenth century

Plate 8
James Pattison Cockburn
St Louis Street, 1829

46. Mrs Louise Watson in her bedroom at
20 Carleton Street, Toronto, c. 1910.

Mrs Louise Watson sits wedged in among the heavy furnishings of
her Toronto bedroom in the 1910 photograph shown in Figure 46.
She had scarcely enough room for a pot of tea let alone a friend to
drink it with.

According to Pocius, bedrooms in Calvert are used simply for
sleeping, in part perhaps because they've been unheated until the
recent past. As such they were the only truly private spaces in the
home, indeed in the whole community. He offers an example to
underscore the point: 'When Larry Sullivan was dying from cancer,
nearby neighbours made sure that someone was there to sit up
with him, even if it was long into the night. At no other time would
a community resident have access to or need to visit the private
space of the bedroom, a room rarely seen by anyone except those
who use it. But sickness transforms this space into a place to visit,
and in this special ritualized visit, access is permitted.'[70]

In the recent past the middle-class bedroom has become an
ever more private place. With its own attached bathroom, telephone, and TV set, the 'main suite' has assumed something of the
character of a self-contained apartment. Walled up in their flat

within a home, middle-class parents have built an unprecedented barrier between themselves and their offspring. It should come as little surprise, then, that their kids have responded in kind. Since the '60s the number of larger homes in Canada has grown while the average number of household residents has shrunk – quite dramatically in fact. One result has been that young children now commonly have a bedroom each, while most adolescents regard this condition as an entitlement, not a privilege. The rooms themselves offer a separate place for schoolwork, and often include radios, televisions, and phones among the many electronic gadgets once available only centrally within the house. The bedroom has become every adolescent's private domain, decorated to her tastes, maintained to her standards of order and cleanliness. It's now a semi-autonomous household space with boundaries as jealously guarded as those of any medieval domain. Once upon a time 'parents keep out' was just a sign children hung on the clubhouse door.

The Apartment

The apartment building arrived in Canada about the turn of the twentieth century, a new dwelling form for a new urban age. Rather late to industrialize, Canada clung to its rural past longer than most Western nations and this slowed the apartment's progress. Slow to develop as well were the vast open spaces surrounding Canadian cities, which kept land costs low and encouraged the sprawl of the single-family dwellings so characteristic of its urban places even today. Thus, while the apartment block established a place for itself in most communities, it did so rather more gradually than in the densely packed cities of western Europe and the eastern American seaboard – London and New York, for example, where the first apartment buildings for a bourgeois market appeared in the mid-nineteenth century.

In 1921, the first year this information was published, only 2 percent of Canadian dwellings were apartments, the largest concentration – some 14 percent – in Montreal. By midcentury one home in four was an apartment of some sort, though most were located in small buildings of just a few units. It wasn't until the great construction boom of the 1960s and 1970s that the large apartment tower flourished, and even then the small apartment building remained the predominant form. At last report only 9 percent of all Canadian homes were in buildings of five storeys or more, while over 30 percent were in smaller complexes. In this, as in so many other aspects of Canadian life, Quebec has always been something of an exception, with its greater commitment to apartment living. The small apartment building has long been especially popular in Montreal; it accounted for a third of all city homes in 1921, and by the early 1990s the proportion had risen to over 60 percent.[71]

From the outset, in English Canada at least, the apartment building was home to the urban middle and upper classes, whose tastes and expectations left their mark on overall building design as well as on the layout of individual units. Early on in the century a few large buildings were built to luxurious standards, very much in the manner of the grand apartment complexes found in great European and American cities. But most apartments had a more modest aim: to reproduce middle-class domestic comforts within a new housing form.[72] In this sense the form distinguished itself from the crowded tenements, barracks, bunkhouses, and workers' lodges that housed so many Canadians from the late nineteenth century onward.

Whatever novelties the apartment block might have offered, in interior spatial design it was a deeply conservative force. The layouts of most suites tried to preserve the basic elements of the single-family home. Interiors were subdivided according to the design principles of the multiroom middle-class dwelling – separate spaces for separate functions, with special pains often taken to set bathing, the toilet, and sleeping quarters apart from the rest of the interior. Corridors linked all rooms, offering ease of movement while preserving the privacy of each chamber. Apartments built for the wealthy occasionally included a maid's room, leading off the kitchen. These design goals were not always easy to achieve, particularly in the early 'experimental' years of the apartment era. Problems of spatial organization occasionally defeated architects, creating suites with inappropriately clustered rooms. In time, however, Canadian apartment designers resolved most of these difficulties and organized interiors in much the same manner as those of freestanding houses.

Figure 44, one wing of an eight-storey Toronto building constructed in 1910, reveals these features clearly. Of the four apartments shown here, two were unusual for they lacked a kitchen (as in some New York apartment complexes intended primarily for bachelors, who presumably dined out). But all four demonstrate the division of space we've come to recognize as a leading characteristic of nineteenth-century home interiors. The Annandale Apartments, a six-storey complex built in Kingston, Ontario, in 1928 possessed the same features (Figure 45). Shown here is one suite on a floor of six two-bedroom units. The larger plan shows a broad central corridor bisecting the floor. Most rooms in the apartments were separate, aligned in a row to maximize window access, the sleeping quarters set well apart from the living and dining rooms while a sun porch added a graceful touch to each unit. But by this time each apartment also bore the imprint of the open plan, the dining, living, and sun rooms separated only by symbolic, partial walls.

Working-class tenements, modest apartments purpose built for labouring families, were an uncommon sight on the Canadian scene. As we've already observed, even people of limited means often lived in detached housing, except in urban Ontario, where semi-detached and row housing flourished, and Quebec, where the plexes prevailed. When the urban poor huddled together they often did so in large older houses subdivided to create a number of small suites. Thus Figure 47, a three-storey Halifax purpose-built tenement constructed in 1909, is something of an exception. But it reveals the same concern for the separation of spaces even within the confines of very modest apartments. Each floor of the building included four suites, with shared toilet and bathing facilities located off the central corridor. The larger apartments (800 square feet or 75 square metres) had four rooms each while the smaller (440 square feet or 40 square metres) held only three, but both sought a maximum of privacy with a minimum of means.

The same conservatism in interior design extended well into the post-Second World War era, during the building boom of the late 1940s and '50s. Although the contemporary demand was greatest for small single-family houses, a surge of small apartment construction also provided inexpensive shelter for tens of thousands of Canadians with modest incomes. The two-bedroom suite illustrated in Figure 48 was located in a large tract of simple but comfortable walk-up apartment houses built in Edmonton during the

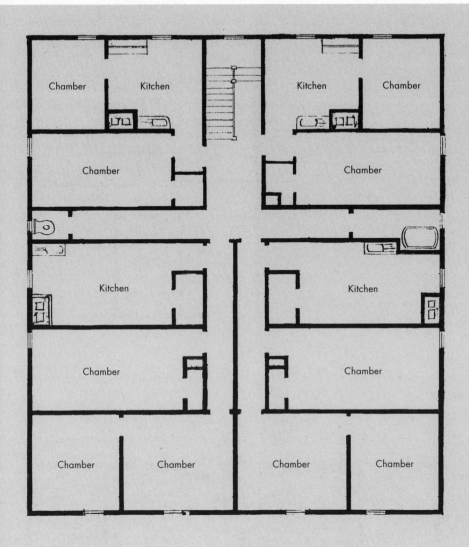

47. Detail of plan for purpose-built tenement building, Halifax, 1906.

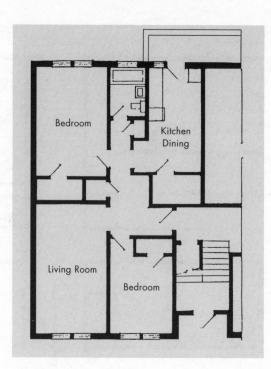

48. Plan for two-bedroom apartment, Edmonton, 1950s.

49. Plan for second floor of apartment house, Ste-Anne-de-Bellevue, Quebec, 1954.

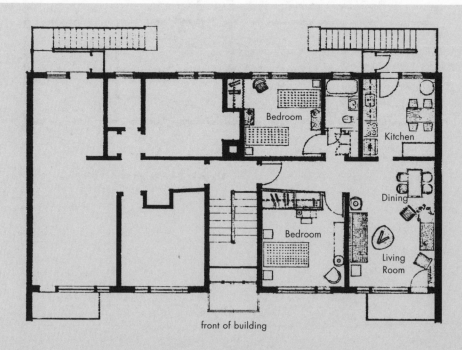

front of building

early '50s. The interior of this 800 square foot (75 square metre) unit, like those of the hundreds of others in the complex, was subdivided in the classic closed form.

Perhaps the sharpest break with traditional housing designs occurred in Quebec, where interiors reflecting national influences quickly displaced the older layouts of the plexes. In terms of their floor plans, at least, small postwar Quebec apartments differed little from those in the rest of the country. Figure 49 depicts the organization of the second floor of a two-storey, four-suite building constructed in 1954 for an investor in Ste-Anne-de-Bellevue. Each 900 square foot (184 square metre) unit spanned the building from front to back, its two bedrooms and bathroom set apart from the kitchen, dining, and living rooms – here organized as one continuous space. Each also boasted a small balcony, the most forward-looking design innovation in the building. Soon apartments from coast to coast, great and small, extruded carbuncles like these.

It was the highrise apartment, however, that brought the ultimate triumph of open planning to the Canadian home, in the process imposing its principles on most forms of popular housing across the country. During the 1960s and '70s the number of apartments in Canada almost trebled, from 750,000 to 2,100,000.[75] Much of this expansion was due to the boom in highrise construction in city centres and suburbs alike. Big cities saw the most vigorous growth because high land prices encouraged developers to build up instead of out, but even small ones found their skylines altered by the new apartment tower. The call of modern fashion proved just as irresistible as that of economic benefit when it came to building tall housing blocks. The highrise apartment was an industrial product, mass-produced according to standardized plans. As designers and builders tried to control their costs through the endless quest for efficiencies, they found that open plans suited their needs perfectly. The open plan maximized useful living space by organizing interiors simply, and by dispensing with all but the essentials of the comfortable small home. Not surprisingly, first to go were the long corridors and the separate living and dining rooms so characteristic of the Canadian apartment in its youthful prime.

50. Detail of typical highrise floor plan
with inset balconies, Edmonton, 1962.

We see these innovations in the floor plan of one of the first
multistorey apartment towers built in Edmonton during the early
'60s. Figure 50 depicts the standard design employed for part of
each floor, including examples of one- and two-bedroom and studio apartments. In the former two a galley kitchen was built into
the living and dining space while the bathroom and bedrooms
were enclosed and set apart. A small balcony was also carved from
the open living area. The studio unit was essentially a single space,
with the bathroom and storage areas enclosed at one end. No bal-

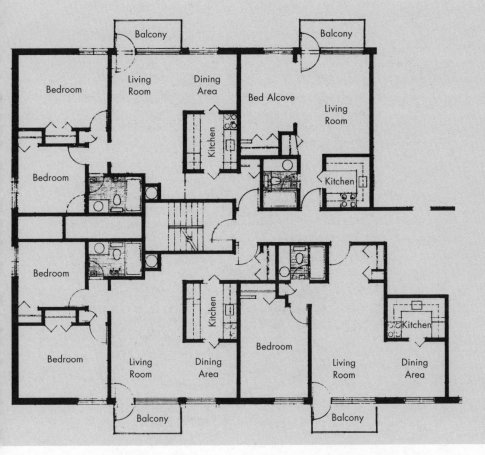

51. Detail of typical highrise floor plan with cantilevered balconies, Hull, Quebec, 1971.

cony was provided, presumably in order not to reduce the already small amount of living space within the suite.

The building in Figure 51 was constructed in Hull, Quebec, in 1971. While the rooms were arranged somewhat differently, the separation of open and closed spaces was essentially that of the Edmonton tower. In spatial terms the only difference between the two was the provision of cantilevered balconies rather than inset ones, allowing the single residents of this building the same access to the great outdoors enjoyed by its happily married residents.

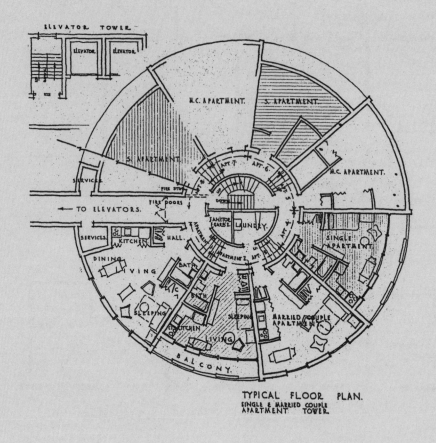

ELEVATOR TOWER.

ELEVATOR   ELEVATOR

M.C. APARTMENT.   S. APARTMENT.

S. APARTMENT.

M.C. APARTMENT.

SERVICES

FIRE STOP

← TO ELEVATORS.   FIRE DOORS

DOWN

JANITOR   LAUNDRY.

SERVICES   KITCHEN   HALL.

DINING   LIVING

SINGLE
APARTMENT

BATH

DINING   LIVING   BATH

KITCHEN   SLEEPING   SLEEPING   MARRIED COUPLE
APARTMENT

LIVING

BALCONY.

TYPICAL FLOOR   PLAN.
SINGLE & MARRIED COUPLE
APARTMENT TOWER.

52. Detail of plan for circular apartment
towers, Frobisher Bay, Baffin Island,
1958.

Nothing at all remains here of Quebec's distinctive architectural traditions. This building could have been built anywhere in Canada – in fact probably just about anywhere in North America.

The apotheosis of the Canadian open plan apartment is found in Figure 52, the 1958 design for a twin tower circular highrise complex proposed for the tiny northern community of Frobisher Bay (now Iqaluit) on Baffin Island. The architect envisioned a series of eight wedge-shaped apartments on each floor, the four larger wedges for childless married couples, the four slightly smaller ones for singles. All units were completely open except for the bathroom, while large balconies were intended for the single residents' suites – an ideal spot to watch the midnight sun in summer and the northern lights in winter. The bizarre character of this fantasy is all too apparent when we compare it with the photograph of the Dick family at home (Figure 4) taken a few months later. The Dicks and their four children then lived in their single-room northern home at the other end of the Northwest Territories, thousands of miles distant. Theirs was a frontier cabin laid out on the 'open plan' but without any of the ideological underpinnings of this modern housing ideal. The cultural gulf between their home life and that envisioned by the designers of postwar highrise apartments is breathtaking. It's a useful reminder of the great diversity of housing conditions that existed at any point in Canada's past. In this case, presumably, the architect had never been north of Ottawa. It would be hard to imagine a less appropriate form for the North than that proposed here, based as it was on the tastes and needs of youthful big city Canadians. We can only hope it was never built.

3 | The House in Its Setting

A dwelling's interior affects the relations of household members with one another much more than it does with the community at large. Its location, on the other hand – its placement vis-à-vis nearby homes, roads, and walkways – shapes relationships between its residents and their neighbours. For this reason we now turn to the setting of the Canadian home, and thus to the boundaries between family space and public space as they've shifted over time.

The Farmhouse

The earliest rural settlers in French Canada built their homes on river lots along the banks of the St Lawrence, the major transportation route in the colony. But after 1700 colonists took up farmlands well away from the river and built roads throughout the colonies to connect their communities. Thus, by the mid-eighteenth century most rural French Canadians lived in small wooden houses beside a road and within sight and sound of their neighbours.[74] Because the land had been divided into long narrow lots, *habitant* dwellings usually stood close to one other, adjacent to and facing the nearest country lane. As a result, ribbons of houses lined both sides of the roadways in most settled districts. Figure 53 illustrates the typical pattern of house placement, though it does not show the lot divisions. An excerpt of a detailed map drawn for General James Murray in 1762, it depicts the road running through the seigneuries of Batiscan and Champlain on the north shore of the St Lawrence River between Trois-Rivières and Quebec City.

The French-Canadian custom of building simple rural homes beside roadways continued throughout the nineteenth century and on into the twentieth. In 1829, the British military artist James

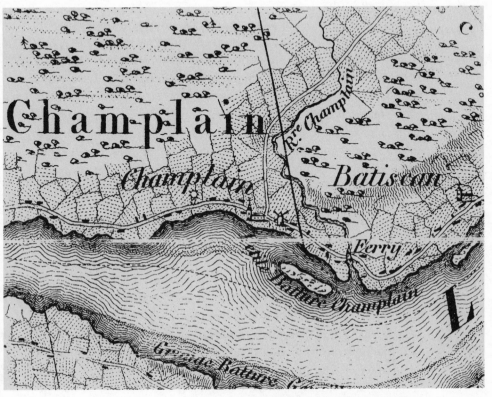

53. Detail of map of Quebec drawn for General James Murray, 1762. The black rectangles on both sides of the roads indicate the location of houses.

Pattison Cockburn captured this feature of habitant dwellings in a watercolour of Point Lévis (Plate 3). This characteristic manner of siting houses prevailed not only in Quebec but in most French settlements in North America, including those in Nova Scotia, Cape Breton, and New Brunswick.

Several British settlements in the Maritimes and Upper Canada shared something of this appearance. Until roads began to link Nova Scotian towns, settlers often built farm dwellings along the shores of the colony. But during the late eighteenth century, when roadways were gradually cut across the peninsula between Halifax, Windsor, and Truro, inland settlers usually located their homes with easy access to them. Yet while some built next to the road, as in the St Lawrence Valley, others placed their homes at a distance from the public thoroughfare. An early survey map of the route from Halifax to Windsor shows some homes positioned immediately beside the road and others set well back from it.[75]

In pioneer Upper Canada the practice varied. Some of the first settlers built their houses immediately by the roadside. Over time, however, the tendency was to build them away from highways. When she first came to Richmond Hill just north of Toronto in the late 1820s, Mary Gapper noted that the new cottages of the district were 'more or less distant from the road.' A midcentury watercolour of a farmstead in Vaughan Township depicts the likely path of development: an older log dwelling abutting the Vaughan Plank Road and a newer, much grander, colonnaded home set back from it, screened by a fence and an evergreen hedge (Plate 4). The farmhouse in the foreground of Plate 5, an anonymous engraving of Guelph published in 1831, was not only built well off the road but facing away from it, too.[76]

If anything Ontario farmhouses moved farther back on their lots, away from roads and highways, as the century progressed. A glance through the county atlases published during the late nineteenth century provides a clue. These books were generously illustrated with the farms of their subscribers, tributes to the ambitions, achievements, and vanities of a prosperous rural population. Conventionally they displayed the farm home in a garden setting, often linked to the passing road by a long, tree-lined driveway and secluded from public view by gracious treed borders. Surviving photographs suggest that sometimes these atlases embellished rural Ontario beyond recognition. The Amaranth Township farm in Figure 54 hadn't been cloaked in romantic excess. It was a utilitarian working farm, its owners' energies all spent on the mundane tasks of their calling. But with no leafy borders to obscure our view, we can clearly see the substantial distance that stood between the farm buildings and the passing road.

The prairie farmhouse of the late nineteenth and early twentieth centuries stood even farther from its neighbours than did its eastern counterparts. The original western surveys established the square mile (more commonly the 'section') as the basic unit of land. Subsequent homestead policy shaped the dispersed pattern of settlement by offering quarter sections to settlers for a small sum as long as they built a home on their land and cultivated a portion of it within three years. When some groups tried to adopt other settlement forms the federal government prevented them. Soon after the turn of the twentieth century, for example, Doukhobor homesteaders in Saskatchewan attempted to build European-style rural villages and to farm their lands communally. But after a few years the Laurier government enforced the homestead law and the experiment collapsed.[77] Government policy, so it seems, decreed that rural homes

54. Homestead of Mr and Mrs Thomas Davis, Amaranth Township, Ontario, 1900.

55. Farmstead near Rowatt,
Saskatchewan, July 1946.

56. Gilbert Berdahl farm, Hesketh,
Alberta, 1960.

would stand farther apart on the prairies than in the rest of Canada. They were also placed a considerable distance from the road, as Figure 55 indicates. This bungalow near Rowatt, Saskatchewan, was a generation old when a National Film Board photographer took the picture in 1946. Yet the windbreak planted around the site had scarcely reached a man's height.

The ideal rural prairie dwelling – the one upheld by progressive agricultural practice – was set off by a front lawn and flower beds, and sheltered from winter's cold and summer's heat by borders of tall trees. This practice could only accentuate the farm family's isolation.[78] Given the length of time it took for most tree species to mature on the open plains, the ideal could only be a distant goal in the early settlement years, but by midcentury it had often been realized. The dramatic 1960 photograph of the Gilbert Berdahl Farm near Hesketh, Alberta, depicts the placement of an established prairie farmstead, surrounded by a mature windbreak that screened the house from the passing road (Figure 56). These features of siting farm dwellings were widely shared on the plains, and emphasized the spaces that set prairie neighbours apart from one another.

Ranch houses in the Alberta foothills were a local variation of the form. The large size of most ranches meant that ranchers' homes usually stood at great distances from one another. Some, like the Hull Ranch house south of Calgary, were nostalgic monuments to the settled domesticity of faraway lands (Figure 57) while others were simple dwellings built with little more than utility in mind (Figure 58). But in this case the extreme isolation of ranch life could encourage uncommonly warm hospitality. Moira O'Neill, an Irish gentlewoman who ranched in Alberta in the late nineteenth century, described her Canadian neighbours as 'unfailing in kindness and hospitality to new-comers.' For her the social life of the ranching frontier replaced the artifice of its British counterpart with openness and warmth.

It is true that we do not scatter cards upon each other or make many afternoon calls, for reasons connected with time and space and other large considerations. We do not give each other dinner-parties either; but we give each other dinner, generally at 1 p.m., and beds for the night. People usually come when they have some reason for passing

57. Hull ranch house, south of Calgary, 1895.

58. Settlers' buildings and cattle on a Bow River horse ranch near Cochrane, Alberta, c. 1890s.

this way; and in a ranching country, houses are so few and far between that hospitality of necessity becomes a matter of course. As a matter of course also, people do not expect to be amused. We have no means of formally entertaining each other, and it is not thought amusing to talk from morning till night. A visitor prefers to smoke his pipe in peace, to find his way out and wander round the corrals, inspect any bit of building that may be going on, or cast a critical eye on the stock. After which he saddles his *cayuse* for himself, and departs on his own affairs.[79]

The Villa

However modest or pretentious the farmhouse might be, the lives it enfolded were focused on rural production. The villa, a familiar but much less common rural house type, served quite different purposes. From its origins in antiquity, the villa has always defined itself in relation to the city: a retreat from urban life, a place for pleasure and relaxation in a rustic setting. Its primary economic ties have seldom been to the countryside, its very existence having always expressed privacy, leisure, wealth, and luxury. As the villa's most persuasive historian has put it, 'the content of villa ideology is rooted in the contrast of country and city, in that the virtues and delights of the one are presented as the antitheses of the vices and excesses of the other.'[80]

Villas first appeared in the British American colonies in the late eighteenth century and they flourished throughout much of the nineteenth. Initially built by a colonial upper class of wealthy merchants, professionals, and administrators, in time they found favour among those of slightly more modest means as well. When passing through Montreal after the War of 1812, John Howison noticed numerous villas built in the English manner on the outskirts of the city, 'the variety and beauty of which, prove the wealth and taste of their owners.'[81] Much later in the century a finely detailed British ordnance survey map recorded several villas and country cottages, each with a characteristic rustic name, dotting the countryside just west of Kingston (Figure 59). While the immediate aesthetic inspiration behind this movement was largely English, the desire to own a country house knew no cultural bounds. Families of British, French, American, and Canadian origin all built villas during these years.

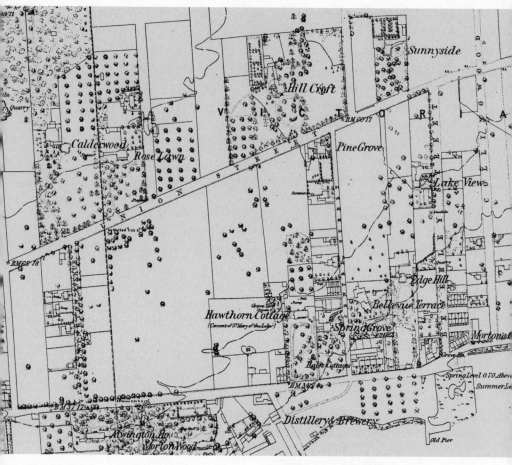

59. Detail of plan of Kingston and its environs, Ontario, 1869.

That of the French-Canadian businessman, educator, writer, politician and office holder Joseph-François Perrault offers a striking example. Perrault's long career extended from the mid-1770s until his death in 1844. He lived most of his later years in a villa on the outskirts of Quebec that he purchased toward the end of the eighteenth century. He called it Aisle Champêtre (Country Retreat), the name expressing the age old cultural and psychological meaning of the villa. According to Perrault's biographer, the Aisle stood atop a hill, surrounded by a four-acre garden and separated from the road by a stone wall topped by wooden railings. The drive from the road to the house was lined with large floral vases and borders that set off the model vegetable and orchard plots gracing the grounds in front of the house. The rear garden featured a pond with waterfowl, turtles, and aquatic plants, as well as luxuriant flower beds.[82] While very much a man of the city, Perrault found his solace in the countryside, surrounded by a natural world that he shaped to his own tastes.

The villas of colonial British America were bucolic variations on the theme of Aisle Champêtre: gracious houses placed in the country and set in gardened surroundings. They differed widely in size and splendour, aesthetic sensibility and architectural style, but invariably they expressed the owner's desire for privacy, ease, and close ties with the world of nature. That of the Halifax merchant John Moody was typical. In the early years of the nineteenth century he built Gorsebrook, a handsome estate just south of the city. A 115-metre stone wall separated the property from the road along its front, while a driveway, lawns, and trees created a dramatic setting for the large two-storey wooden-frame dwelling. Similarly, the Chief Justice of the Court of King's Bench in Lower Canada, James Monk, built a country house near Montreal in the early nineteenth century. It was a stately stone building in the Palladian manner placed in a graceful English parkland setting (Figure 60). Some time during the mid- or late 1830s Captain Thomas Dick, co-owner of a Toronto steam shipping company, built the more modest villa on the city's outskirts shown in Plate 6. Dick's rustic retreat was little more than a simple cottage, but like its more ostentatious counterparts it boasted a luxuriant garden setting. In their various ways each of these dwellings expressed the villa's essence: seclusion, comfort, wealth, repose, and affinity for nature.[83]

60. George Heriot, *Monkville near Montreal*, 1813.

While the villa's most enduring attraction was its appeal to anti-urban sentiments, those attracted to it took little interest in the exertions of rural life. In putting the urban community behind them villa dwellers usually embraced a life lived in domesticated nature, relying on incomes from rents, investments, and assorted urban callings to support their rural idyll. The ideological features of the villa home were articulated much more clearly during the second half of the century than the first, when urban growth, the accumulation of middle-class wealth, and the development of commuter railways encouraged the move to the suburbs, reducing the social exclusiveness of villa development in the process. Not surprisingly, some of the villa's most eloquent advocates were real-estate promoters, who skilfully exploited age old myths of an idealized country life for their own profit. Still, their assertions spoke to widely shared convictions about the villa's enduring cultural values.

In 1856, the Toronto real-estate broker John Maulson advertised a suburban village development midway between Weston and Balmoral, two villages northwest of the city and recently linked to it by rail. On offer were sixty-nine 'villa park lots,' ranging in size from 0.6 to seven acres, most of them abutting Balmoral Avenue, a proposed tree-lined boulevard and the intended axis of the community. Maulson's pitch touched on the time-honoured themes of the realtor's promotion, especially the profits and pleasures of owning rather than renting. But he saved his most fulsome praise for the superior virtues of life in the country over that in the city: the blessings of fresh air, grass, and trees; the pleasures of raising fruits and vegetables, milk and eggs; the better health enjoyed by the country dweller; and – most of all – the moral superiority of rural living. In terms harking back over the long ideological history of the villa he concluded:

> To men familiar with city noise and activity, the quiet country often seems sluggish and monotonous. Unhappy they who have become unable to appreciate the power and beauty of repose! Be assured that in these calm scenes may be found a peace and joy unknown to the restless town. In the culture of domestic affections; in training your children to habits of industry, learning, and goodness; in reading and reflection; in the pleasant toils of the garden; in social intercourse with

your neighbours; and in good offices to all who need them – you will find healthful and delightful occupations for every hour which you are permitted to pass at home. This is not an imaginary picture. The experiment has been tried by thousands who are now enjoying its fruits. Men, women, and children who once wilted and pined among stones and bricks in the close city air, but who now luxuriate among trees and grass and flowers, and feasting upon their own unbought dainties, are happier than kings.[84]

Maulson and his kind were the villa's chief apologists throughout the rest of the century.

During the late nineteenth century and the first half of the twentieth, the Canadian villa took three distinct paths. The one straight on led to the monumental summer houses of the rich, in keeping with a tradition by then at least two millennia old.[85] A second turned gently in the direction of the summer cottage, that simple, modest, almost democratic country dwelling that allowed growing numbers of Canadians to own holiday homes in rural or wilderness landscapes. The third veered more sharply toward the suburban house, the freestanding single-family home aloof on its own lot and enfolded by lawns and gardens. But here we leap ahead of ourselves for, before we arrive in the suburbs, we need to retrace our steps and examine the house in its urban setting.

The Home in City and Suburb

Towns and cities in colonial British America were densely built places. Buildings usually stood cheek by jowl abutting the street. In an age when workplace and dwelling place were often one and the same, urban centres weren't nearly as segregated by social and economic function as they've become. Workshops and stores, churches and government offices mingled with houses in compact diversity. These features of urban design were as characteristic of pioneer villages and small towns in 1800 as they were of incipient cities in the same era, and in one form or another they persisted for most of the century.

An anonymous early-nineteenth-century sketch of Montreal offers an illustration (Plate 7). We see the city's stone and wood buildings with their steep-pitched shingle roofs crowded up against one another and pressing in on the street, a confusion of urban forms and functions. The many watercolours in James Cockburn's Quebec City albums convey the same impression, for example his view of St Louis Street painted in 1829 (Plate 8). Here is one of the city's narrow streetscapes, the buildings abutting one another in a discontinuous line, their steps descending directly onto the cobbled sidewalk. A lithograph of Digby, Nova Scotia, printed during the 1830s or 1840s, reveals the same clustering beside the road running through this small Maritime town (Figure 61).

61. M.G. Hall, *View of Digby, Nova Scotia*, early nineteenth century.

The first age of photography displayed this feature of urban places even more vividly. Figures 62 and 63 are among the earlier surviving photographs of any Canadian city. They depict the Toronto skyline on a warm afternoon in early spring in 1856. Two of a series of panoramic shots taken from a hotel rooftop near the city centre, they illustrate that mingling of new and old, wealth and poverty, commerce and manufacturing, bureaucracy and domesticity so characteristic of the nineteenth-century city. They also offer glimpses into the mid-nineteenth-century uses of urban space: wide streets and narrow lanes, rows of mixed-use buildings next to the sidewalks, and small back yards filled with a disarray of sheds, piles of lumber, and refuse.

Row houses like those in Figure 63 became a fixture in much of urban English Canada during the middle and later years of the century, as did semi-detached dwellings. The number of houses in a row varied, as did their size and decor, for they housed both well-to-do and labouring families. But in their diversity they shared a number of important features, among them direct access to the street, party wall construction, and a multistorey arrangement of rooms. The midcentury Toronto row houses seen here were built without a setback, masking from the public eye the usual jumble of outbuildings behind them. Toward the end of the century the Toronto row house began to edge back from the street line, at least in districts where the well-to-do lived, but the rear yard was still usually reserved for mundane household services. In Montreal during these years the terrace – two or three apartments stacked atop one another, one per floor – was by far the most popular housing form. But multistorey row houses could be found there too, modest homes lining some streets beyond the old city core, more elaborate ones nestled in its gracious English quarters.[86]

Suburban development paced urban growth in the major colonial cities from the mid-eighteenth century on. Quebec's population spilled over its town walls during the French regime, creating the first Canadian suburb, Saint-Roch. The same process commenced in late-eighteenth-century Montreal, when urban expansion burst the city's walls. From then on suburbanization became a permanent feature of civic growth in Canada, as larger cities relentlessly colonized their surrounding countryside. Seen in terms of the

62. Looking north from King and York
Streets, Toronto, 1856. Osgoode Hall
stands at the end of the street.

63. Looking north from King and York Streets, Toronto, 1856.

64. (facing page) Faubourg Saint-Jean in winter, Quebec City, 1872.

placement of houses and the general shape of outdoor domestic space, most nineteenth-century suburbs owed less to their rural settings than to their urban roots. Homes in early suburban Lower Canada, too, were built near the road and close to one another.

Throughout the century suburbia expanded around Canadian cities and towns, and when they swallowed their older suburbs new ones sprang up to replace them. Despite some dramatic innovations in housing form, the customary ways of placing urban houses on lots persisted in outlying Montreal, Quebec, and Trois-Rivières during the mid- and late nineteenth century. French Canada continued to build its suburban and village houses in the time-honoured urban manner – adjacent to the road and abutting one another.[87] The photograph in Figure 64, a winter street scene in Quebec City's Faubourg Saint-Jean in 1872, offers a clear example.

We see the same characteristics in Figure 65, a turn-of-the-century photograph of old Sillery, one of the city's more prosperous districts. Montreal's housing terraces were built in the same fashion and, in some parts of the city, the practice continued into the early twentieth century. Figure 66, a sketch of a typical late-nineteenth-century streetscape published in the 1937 enquiry into working-class housing conditions, portrays the characteristic pattern of 'multiplex' housing fronting the sidewalk, the backs of lots used for fuel sheds, stables, and garages.

In the late nineteenth century, however, a new suburban spatial arrangement began to emerge, rather earlier in English Canada than in Quebec and much like contemporary American and British colonial developments. In contrast to all that had gone before, the house was set back from street and well away from the dwellings on either side. The upper-middle-class suburb established the norm: large houses bordered by lawns and gardens, well removed from sidewalks and roadways and separated from neighbouring dwellings by a hedge, a fence, or a wall. Ottawa's MacLaren Street (Figure 67), a leafy avenue south of Parliament Hill near the Rideau Canal, was one of many such neighbourhoods built at the time. Once adopted, this spatial arrangement was duplicated in big-city and small-town Canada, and it penetrated deeply into the nation's social structure. Modest middle- and working-class subdivisions came to share the same basic pattern as that of the more prosperous suburbs, though on a reduced scale. The size of houses and of the spaces between them asserted the relative wealth of their owners.

At first this new spatial order spread unevenly across the country, but in time it became the dominant practice from coast to coast. It expanded rapidly during great building boom after 1900, leaving large, indelible marks on the old cities of Ontario and even larger ones on Winnipeg, Vancouver, and the other new western cities, where suburban expansion overwhelmed the small, late-Victorian urban communities of the region. By the interwar years the individual house surrounded by gardens had also won some acceptance in suburban Montreal. Figure 68, an aerial view of the city's periphery taken just after the First World War, indicates that the new form had already begun to displace the long-standing practice

65. A street in old Sillery, Quebec City, c. 1900.

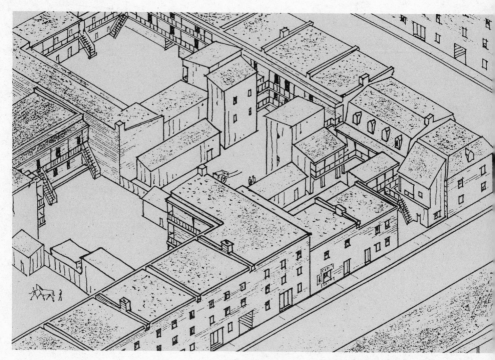

66. Typical late-nineteenth-century
working-class Montreal streetscape.

MACLAREN STREET. OTTAWA.

67. MacLaren Street, Ottawa, late nineteenth century.

of building rows of adjoining homes along the street line. The new suburban plan imprinted its image on Atlantic Canada, too. When north Halifax was rebuilt after the 1917 explosion, the experimental Hydrostone development – row housing based on contemporary British town-planning principles – captured most of the public attention. But the great bulk of replacement housing was based on the ideal of the detached single-family dwelling.[88]

This principle dominated urban and suburban house building across the country until well after midcentury, as typical of low-income housing projects as it was of those for the wealthy. Burkeville, for instance, was an instant working-class suburb built in wartime Vancouver that featured houses laid out in neat rows, each clearly separated from the other and sporting large front and back lawns (Figure 69). Figure 70, a comfortable 1960s scene in Stratford, Ontario, is a typical middle-class manifestation of this trend, down to the broad, featureless front lawn that demanded endless attention. You can almost hear the power mower drone. Twentieth-century suburban design achieved its ultimate expression in Pointe-Claire (Montreal), Don Mills (Toronto), and the British Properties (North Vancouver), quintessential upper-middle-class Canadian suburbs of the post-Second World War era.

This arrangement of urban spaces certainly owed something to the private choices of land owners and home builders. Some early towns in Atlantic Canada were what geographers call 'agglomerated' – an unlovely term meaning clustered. The houses in these communities were set on their plots in whatever manner their builders saw fit, with no particular regard for their alignment with neighbouring dwellings.[89] In many cases the view from the house was the most important factor in determining its location.

But in the long run a variety of town-planning processes played the leading role in deciding where urban homes were built on their lots and positioned in relation to one another. In colonial Canada, unlike early modern Europe, land was concentrated in the hands of the state, not a feudal landowning class. As a result institutions, rather than private individuals, drew up the first plans for most townsites in French and English Canada alike. From the early seventeenth century until well into the nineteenth, government and military officials were the leading Canadian town planners. In the

68. Aerial view of a Montreal area, 1919.

69. Burkville, Richmond, BC, 1942-3.

70. (facing page, bottom) A typical middle-class residential street, Stratford, Ontario, August 1961.

late nineteenth century that role passed to the major railway companies, especially in northern Ontario and Quebec, and in the four western provinces. The Canadian Pacific Railway was probably the greatest town planner in Canada between 1880 and 1930, the most explosive years of urban growth in the nation's history. The city cores created in this fashion usually set the pattern for later expansion, when the owners of adjacent land subdivided their property and sold smaller parcels for building lots.[90]

Almost invariably those who planned towns chose the grid as the basic form, an ancient pattern widely used throughout the Americas from the earliest days of new world settlement. Easy to understand, simple to design, and flexible to implement, it exerted a powerful hold over the bureaucratic mind, reflecting an urge to order and categorize the city. Quebec City was a partial exception. By the turn of the eighteenth century the lower town at the foot of the cliff had grown into a densely built grid, and the Faubourg Saint-Roch later became one on the heights. But those parts of the town lying inside the walls revealed a slightly freer play of forms, even though the straight line held sway there too. The plan for the Town of Niagara, now Niagara-on-the-Lake, drawn up in the 1780s was much more characteristic (Figure 71). With its square blocks of land and its perfectly straight streets, it looks like an early lesson in a short course for apprentice draftsmen. To glance at it you'd never know that the most famous view in North America was just a few miles away. By the late nineteenth century the gridiron had also overtaken some of the clustered settlements in Atlantic Canada, as a bird's eye view of Lunenburg indicates (Figure 72). Here, too, the rectangular layout conceded nothing to the local landscape.[91]

In fact, the list of Canadian cities with non-gridded centres is a very short one indeed, for the straight line and right angle have always been the main design elements of our urban places. Notable early-twentieth-century exceptions were not urban cores at all but pleasant, big-city suburbs such as Vancouver's Shaughnessy and Calgary's Mount Royal, laid out for the wealthy and based on the aesthetic principles of the contemporary British garden city movement. Their curving streets, open spaces, bowered walkways, and cottage-style architectural idiom – what architectural historian Spiro Kostof has called the 'planned picturesque' – tried to bring the

Presbyterian
Church.

Inn

Town of Niagara

Court House
Session

Receiving
Ground

Vineyard

English Church

71. Detail of plan of Town of Niagara,
1787.

72. Detail of bird's eye view of Lunenburg, Lunenburg County, Nova Scotia, 1879.

countryside into the city.[92] In modified form these layouts became rather more common after the Second World War, when crescents and cul-de-sacs replaced straight lines in many suburban developments, softening some of the gridiron's hard edges. Once more the districts designed for the upper middle class showed the way – like Edmonton's Windsor Park – but in time even the working poor could aspire to a house on a curved and treed suburban street, now bearing a more imposing name such as 'drive' or 'court' or 'mews.' Yet the grid persists as a core element of contemporary town-planning principles for it remains visible in the newer suburbs of the nation's major cities. While graceful curves may define the profile of individual suburban streets, more often than not the layout of entire neighbourhoods, as well as the expressways that link them, still bears the mark of the grid.

If the town plan was the primary influence on siting urban homes, municipal regulation played a growing role as well. At first, however, its influence was indirect. In cities and towns built largely of wood – as most Canadian communities were well into the nineteenth century – local governments were more concerned with fire prevention than any other aspect of construction. In Montreal, for instance, two disastrous fires in 1850 and 1852 led city officials to require a solid brick or stone firewall running front to back for every twenty-five feet (eight metres) of a new house's width. Because such walls were costly, the effect of these by-laws was to limit building widths and encourage the construction of duplexes instead of the larger tenements common in eastern American cities.[93] Once these minimum requirements were met, however, decisions about locating houses on lots were left to builders and clients.

But after the turn of the century municipal governments began to intervene more directly in the process of siting urban homes. City governments in Calgary and Edmonton passed their first housing ordinances at the peak of the prewar building boom, at a time when other large Canadian cities were taking similar steps. These by-laws attempted to control such things as lot sizes and building site coverage in addition to prescribing minimum setbacks from the lot lines on all sides.[94] We shouldn't think that these rules were always followed, or even systematically enforced. But from this time local governments took a more active part in shaping the streetscapes of their communities.

Figure 73, an aerial view of the Danforth Avenue-Playter Boulevard area in Toronto, shows the result – a highly uniform pattern of housing placement imposed on a grid. Over time building regulations grew in number, complexity, and restrictiveness. The curved streets of some midcentury suburbs gradually muted the grid's rigid lines, but the mounting requirements of building by-laws had the opposite effect, producing tracts of similar houses on identical lots with identical setbacks, identical heights and, often, identical roof lines. The resulting uniformity echoed that of the grid whether an elegant arc blessed the street or not. We see the results on Waterloo Street in River Heights, one of Winnipeg's perfectly flat (and ironically named) new suburbs in 1946 (Figure 74). In this case the location is almost irrelevant. This scene is so typical that not only the streetscape but the street and district names could be found in cities from coast to coast.

Yet despite the spreading conviction that the family home on its gardened lot was the birthright of all urban Canadians, such dwellings haven't always been as common as we might expect. The proportion of freestanding single-family houses has varied considerably by region as well as by city. The sharp historical divide between French and English Canada is the best-known difference, for the proportion of detached houses has always been much lower in Quebec's cities and towns than in the rest of the country.[95] Only one of every four residences in Montreal and Quebec City were classic North American garden homes during the 1920s, compared to nearly 90 percent in Winnipeg and Vancouver. But the contrast was not just between two primary cultural groups. The smaller proportion of freestanding houses was very much a big-city phenomenon. Conditions in Toronto and Montreal, the country's two largest cities, were roughly similar during the '20s, when most smaller urban places in English Canada had far higher ratios of freestanding homes.

Not only that but the detached house has been in slow retreat through the twentieth century. In 1921, the first year for which this information exists, 85 percent of houses in Canada were single and detached. By 1991 the proportion had declined by a third to 57 percent.

73. Aerial view of Toronto, 1919-20. Danforth Avenue centre bottom, intersected by Playter Boulevard and, above, Jackman Avenue.

74. Row of houses on Waterloo Street,
River Heights, Winnipeg, July 1946.

One obvious reason has been the ongoing march of urbanization. Rural dwellings have almost always stood alone, and as the proportion of rural dwellers has declined so has the dominant house type.

But the underlying explanation seems a good deal more complex. In the four largest Canadian urban areas less than half the housing stock in 1991 consisted of detached single-family dwellings. In the next six largest the proportion was no more than 60 percent.[96] High land and construction costs, increasingly varied zoning requirements, and ever more exacting building codes have combined with shifts in consumer tastes and incomes to undermine the suburban housing ideal. The myth of the dream house may well be intact, but in practice the garden home now glorified in advertisements for life insurance, lawn mowers, and exterior paint is a declining phenomenon. More compact styles of living still meet stiff popular resistance rooted in cultural, economic, and political considerations. The belief in the intrinsic merit of the owner-occupied home, especially strong in English Canada, is bound up with the fact that a house is an important capital investment – the most valuable asset that many families own. In turn these factors are reflected in suburban zoning laws that often encourage large lots, national tax policies that favour home ownership, and a host of other influences that encourage urban sprawl. Still, the townhouse and the apartment now seem the way of the future for city cores. The trend to greater density has even touched the suburbs over the past two or three decades.

The history of siting the Canadian house is a complex tale. Yet for all the diversity of settings one broad trend is evident. From the eighteenth century to at least the mid-twentieth, the dwelling migrated back from the road and in from the sides of its lot. Farmhouse, city house, merchant's villa, or worker's cottage, all shared something of this evolution. This process moved at differing rates in various parts of the country, responding to various social, economic, and cultural forces. Urban places evolved as multilayered collections of housing forms. At any time they usually included homes placed in several fashions. The longevity of many buildings meant that older and newer dwellings coexisted, leaving a rich texture of outdoor domestic spaces, a record of evolving views about appropriate housing placement. Still, time saw the triumph of the suburban ideal. By the early twentieth century the detached family house centred on its own well-groomed lot had become the dominant housing form in urban and suburban Canada. If time has gradually eroded its primacy since then, its image remains deeply embedded in our archetypes of the home, as well as our house building practices today.

The key to understanding the significance of this change lies in the meanings of the spaces surrounding the home. Indoors lay private space, that belonging to the household – the family members, servants, and boarders who lived in the dwelling. The road or street was public space, accessible to all. The area between was transitional, claimed and used by household members but open to the informal scrutiny of neighbours, friends, and strangers.[97] The gardens and yards surrounding a dwelling, like the porches attached to it, formed part of a household's terrain but they also stood open to public view. Activities in these spaces thus combined private and public elements. The summer courtship that flowered on a leafy front verandah was an intensely private affair, but it ripened under the watchful gaze of public opinion. Homes built next to sidewalks, streets, or roadways had no transitional spaces before them. The threshold marked the boundary between private and public terrain; moving indoors or out meant passing directly from one sphere to the other. Row and terrace housing seldom had transitional zones in front or back and almost never on either side. Here only a thin line divided public from private space.

The gradual migration of the house on its lot redrew the borders between private and public in nineteenth- and twentieth-century Canadian domestic life. Placed immediately on the roadside, early country dwellings did without much of the privacy that later rural homes possessed. They particularly lacked that shared space where the community and the household could oversee social activities together. The same was even more true of early town and city homes. As the urban house drew back from the public thoroughfare its privacy increased. No longer set apart from the community by the mere width of a door, the home became buffered by a protective area that shielded it from non-household members. Often its grounds were defined by a fence or hedge marking the divide between inclusion and exclusion. The front yard of the urban dwelling became a zone of potential sociability, a place where families might share a sense of community with friends and neighbours and yet be at home on their own property. The path from the front door to the street led from the private to the public domain. Thus, as the ideal suburban home expanded its dominion during the twentieth century, the amount of privacy available to the Canadian household increased apace. The rich were the greatest beneficiaries, for they could afford the largest spaces and greatest isolation for their homes, followed by the middle class with their more modest properties. The poor, by contrast, benefited least.

The Front of the House

What makes the front of a house the front? At first glance the answer seems so obvious that you'd wonder why anyone would ask. After all, it's common sense that houses normally have a front, a back, and two sides. But why do we call one the front while labelling the others the sides and the back? Some architectural theorists suggest that we identify our homes with our bodies. According to Kent Bloomer and Charles Moore the single-family home is like us, freestanding, the front its face, the hearth its heart, the rear its waste disposal zone, and so on.[98] Yi-Fu Tuan suggests something of the home's psychological resonance. 'An inclination to identify the house and its contents with the human body and soul,' he speculates, 'might have deep roots in the human psyche':

> Freud's conception of the human personality seems grounded in the structure of the bourgeois house. Thus the cellar is the id, the dark ground of being, the place of the furnace that fuels the passions. The living room is the ego, the public and social self. The attic is the superego, dream place for the poet and the introspective child ... Jung took the vertical section of a typical middle-class house ... as a representation of his psyche, the levels of the house being the levels of his consciousness.[99]

Fascinating though these musings may be, they stand a pace or two apart from everyday life. I think we can approach this question in a rather more practical way by considering it both from the viewpoint of someone outside the home and from that of someone within it. To the outsider the front is the social face of the dwelling, the side overlooking the public thoroughfare. It normally includes the entrance used by strangers and others who only occasionally enter the dwelling. The back is the opposite side, perhaps less formal in appearance, certainly more private, normally accessible only to household members, close friends and relations, and service personnel. It's usually associated with the household's more mundane affairs. If the back looks toward a road, as it does in many urban areas, usually this is a lane or alley, a corridor for services such as garbage pickup or, in the now misty past, milk and bread delivery. To put it in the simplest – perhaps a bit too simplistic – terms, front equals public, back equals private.

Seen from inside the dwelling the definitions of front and back become a bit more complex. The same front/back, public/private elements shape our understanding, but their meanings have attached themselves to particular rooms in some times and places and not in others. In the nineteenth-century Toronto row house, for example, the parlour (the home's most public room) stood at the front of the first storey, adjacent to the front entrance, while the kitchen occupied the rear of the same floor next to the back door, a zone reserved for family members and, perhaps, servants (Figures 15 and 18). A century later the front and only door to the Saskatoon row house in Figure 24 opened into the vestibule between the living room on the right and the kitchen on the left. Here front and back seem to have less sharply defined meanings, at least as far as room function is concerned.

In other cases notions of front and back are related to what is considered the most important view from the house. Until the mid-twentieth century houses in most cities and towns were almost invariably placed with no regard for their views; the fronts of most homes just stared at one another across the street. The early-twentieth-century homes built on the slopes of my Vancouver neighbourhood, Point Grey, are a case in point. They were sited according to the demands of a grid, though some of North America's most dramatic urban vistas were begging to be seen – Burrard Inlet, Stanley Park, English Bay, and the north shore mountains. Houses built on the south side of the street faced north and took in the view by accident; they stood a little higher than the houses across the road and so could enjoy the panorama over their roofs. Those standing on the north side looked south. They had a similar height advantage over the dwellings downhill behind them but, facing the street, they saw little more than the sloping lawns and stone retaining walls of their southern neighbours. The best views of the harbour and mountains from some of these houses were to be had from the bathroom window.

As always, there were exceptions. Ranch houses built in the Alberta foothills at the height of the Canadian cattle frontier around the turn of the twentieth century were often placed to take advantage of their prospect.[100] The wealthy, better able to indulge their aesthetic fancies, were inclined to keep vistas in mind when buying property and building homes, especially during our century. Unlike Vancouver, most Canadian towns and cities offered few possibilities for dramatic views, but even a wooded park, a shallow ravine, or a river bend might offer an appealing view. (In recent years golf courses have been added to the list.) Upper-class British immigrants seemed particulary imbued with a taste for picturesque settings, as we can still see in the many well-sited homes on the heights and shorelines of Victoria, which have commanding views of the nearby straits and distant mountains. But the practice of locating homes to take advantage of a vista was fairly uncommon before the mid-twentieth century, and though it grew more popular from that point on it still remained largely a privilege of the well-to-do. In most of these cases the front of the house was the side with the special view.

In some communities, however, residents have wanted views for much more practical reasons. Gerald Pocius tells us that homes in the fishing town of Calvert are placed so that they give their owners a clear view of the sea and the road, the major sources of community news.[101] The people of Calvert live in a highly oral culture, in which exchanging information is a staple of everyday life – community news, the comings and goings of friends and neighbours, the daily round of activities, the success of the catch, and so on. The kitchen being the most important room in the house, homes are built to provide it with a view of the bay or the road, preferably both if at all possible. In this case the kitchen stands at the front of the house, or rather the kitchen defines where the front lies.

A further ambiguity about front and back has emerged in

recent decades as houses in many new suburbs have shifted their focus from the street and front yard to the back yard or garden. The architectural historian Annmarie Adams noted this reorientation in a study of mass-produced California suburban homes put up by a merchant builder during the 1960s.[102] Each house offers a blank façade to the street, its most heavily used interior space a multi-purpose room featuring floor to ceiling windows overlooking lawns and gardens on the opposite side of the dwelling and surrounded by high wood fences. The architectural intent, she suggests, was to ensure 'that family life was focused within the property lines of the suburban home.'

The house in the Edmonton suburb of Mill Woods (Figure 75), built in 1979, is a typical Canadian example. The most prominent feature of its façade is the two-door built-in garage, the home's 'front' entrance tucked away to one side under a small roof extension, while two bedroom windows survey a large expanse of concrete driveway. It doesn't take much to imagine a basketball hoop nailed above the garage doors. No service lane runs behind this house, so the street offers the only public approach to the dwelling. In this as in so many other newer suburban homes, the front of the house has migrated to the back, the living and dining rooms cut off from the street by the garage as well as the kitchen, bathroom, and bedrooms. With no back lane the garden enjoys a new exclusiveness. Here the life of the household is directed away from public space, the street, toward the ever greater privacy of the garden.

Like many innovations in the use of domestic space, the recent *volte-face* of the suburban home stems in part from changes in popular taste. Tens of thousands of new home buyers have simply preferred fashionable back-facing houses to traditionally oriented ones. In part it also reflects a desire to contain development costs by reducing the amount of land absorbed by streets and lanes. But by far the most fundamental cause lies in the massive reorientation in suburban life caused by the rise of the automobile.

Although the auto arrived in Canada early in the twentieth century, at the same time as in most of the Western world, it didn't become a mass consumption good until after the Second World War. But then the change was swift. There were four times as many cars on the nation's roads in 1975 as there had been in 1950, one for

75. House in Mill Woods, Edmonton, 1979.

every two Canadians of driving age as opposed to one in five. The auto assumed a central, perhaps *the* central, place in city planning during these years. Cars collapsed distances in the peripheries of cities, making it possible to extend garden suburbs farther and farther into the countryside. With these changes came the decentralization of urban services and their move to areas easily accessible by car. Shopping malls and business strips, built beside major highways and surrounded by acres of parking, became new centres of suburban life, the auto the link with the family home. Like so many homes of this era, the Mill Woods house gave pride of place to the car, the most important of all household appliances – even to the point of inviting it indoors.

Porches, Verandahs, Patios, Decks

Porches and verandahs are part of the house but they also lie outside it. Located along one or more of its outer walls, they're covered by a roof but usually remain open to the elements on at least one side. Most often they shelter the entrance to a home as well. The two terms have somewhat different meanings in Britain and North America. Here we use them almost interchangeably, though we normally consider the porch smaller than the verandah, and I propose to use them in this manner in what follows. In British usage a verandah is largely a feature of domestic architecture but a porch might also mean a portico or colonnade or cloister attached to a larger, more public building. Architectural historians have filled long pages with their reflections on the verandah, emphasizing its colonial origins and its close association with the bungalow.[103] We needn't repeat that discussion here but it's useful to note that the concept of the porch has its roots in ancient Greece and has been embedded in the English language for a very long time. Verandah, in contrast, is a relative newcomer, introduced from India early in the eighteenth century.

From our perspective porches and verandahs are important because these structures form a bridge between indoors and outdoors, between the life of the home and that of the community. For this reason they combine private with public elements. They form part of the dwelling to which they're attached and so extend its living space out of doors. At the same time, lacking closed-in walls they're open to the neighbours' gaze. Someone passing a warm summer's eve on their front porch is at home but in public at the same time.

Before the late nineteenth century many – perhaps most – small Canadian homes lacked a porch, at least in urban places. We certainly see none in Cockburn's watercolour of St Louis Street in 1829 (Plate 8). Nor were there any on rue Saint-Augustin, a modest Quebec City suburban street in 1859 (Figure 76). The objects extending over the Toronto sidewalk in the 1856 photograph in Figure 63 were awnings, not porches. From the midcentury on, working-class housing in Montreal sprouted back porches or galleries on the upper storeys, but these served only to connect apartments with the stairways that led to assorted outhouses and storage sheds in the back yards. The front porches and outdoor iron stairways now so characteristic a feature of east end Montreal didn't make their appearance till toward the end of the century, when builders started to place houses some distance back from the lot line. Porches and staircases soon filled these empty spaces and, by relocating stairways out of doors, saved valuable indoor space.[104] The architectural historian Jean-Claude Marsan suggests that Montreal builders thought porches necessary because the houses they constructed were intended for migrants from the countryside, where verandahs were common.

But the porch has long been a common feature of more elaborate houses. Ones like the dignified Palladian portico on Monkville (Figure 60) were characteristic of houses built on classical British models from the late eighteenth century throughout most of the nineteenth. The verandah also made its appearance by name early on in the century. In 1832, Mary Gapper and her new husband Edward O'Brien placed one along three sides of the new home they constructed overlooking Kempenfeldt Bay on Lake Simcoe.[105] That on Captain Dick's rustic 1830s country cottage extended the full length of the house front (Plate 6). Verandahs were particularly common on larger houses until after the turn of the twentieth century. The plans for William Allen's extravagant home in midcentury suburban Toronto (Figure 12) reveal a broad verandah running the length of one side of the house, and most of its breadth at the back as well.

76. A view of rue Saint-Augustin at the intersection of rue Nouvelle, Quebec City, 1859.

Queen Anne Revival houses, a style that flourished during the decades leading up to the First World War, often featured elaborate curved verandahs like that on the front of Mr Black's Ottawa home around the turn of the century (Figure 77). Even very modest dwellings might have a simple verandah. They were common in turn-of-the-century small-town and suburban Quebec (Figure 65), where they sometimes lacked even a railing. Indeed verandahs were found in rural and small-town homes everywhere in central and eastern Canada. They were also a characteristic feature of the California bungalows so widely built in western Canada during the great building boom just before the outbreak of the First World War. The speculative Calgary properties built by Messrs Robertson and Carlile around 1912 were typical of the type (Figure 78).

But after the war the verandah quickly fell from fashion, to be replaced by a much more modest variation – sometimes little more than a covered stoop. Many existing verandahs were glassed in to keep the cold at bay, drawing this space back inside the house and extending the months of the year it could be used. As for new houses, popular designs from the 1920s onward often provided nothing more than a set of stairs up to a small covered landing just outside the front door. Usually these offered scarcely enough space for a single folding chair let alone the suites of comfortable outdoor furniture that had once dignified the nation's better verandahs (Figure 74). The utilitarian low-rental housing units built in Drumheller, Alberta, in the late 1960s (Figure 79) represent the furthest extreme, stripped of all excess to pare construction costs to the utmost. Here only the hint of a porch roof is visible. Given the winds that often blow through this small prairie city the only cover such shelters might offer would be to nesting birds.

Since the glory days of the verandah, in fact, the suburban home has turned its back on the street. From the mid-twentieth century on, in particular, the patio, deck, and poolside have supplanted the verandah or porch as the zone of outdoor sociability. In time the auto usurped the street, which gradually devoted itself to parking and to fast, efficient transport. On their part pedestrians found streets rather less welcoming, and perhaps less safe, with passing time. In the older immigrant quarters of our larger cities today, notably Toronto and Montreal, verandahs remain centres of

77. The Black family garden and house, Ottawa, c. 1900.

78. Row of houses in Calgary, c. 1912.

79. Low-rental housing, Drumheller, Alberta, 1969.

neighbourliness and the evening streets fill with people out for a stroll – at least in the warmer months. After the Second World War many newcomers brought old world patterns of outdoor sociability to their new Canadian homes, reviving a street life by then almost vanished from the nation's spreading suburbs. Still, whether or not we may be blessed with a verandah, most of us would never dream of sitting out front on a warm summer's eve to chat with passers-by. Some of them are joggers bent on improving their cardiovascular systems, while most of the rest pass by far too quickly, their car windows tightly closed so that the air conditioning will work. Outdoor domesticity has retreated to the other side of the house, where family and invited friends can enjoy a leisurely chat or a casual meal in the privacy of the garden.

Gardens and Yards

When I studied in England in the late 1960s a friend invited me to visit his parents' home in the leafy London suburb of St John's Wood. He showed me around their house, airy, comfortable, and gracious but in no way ostentatious, a fitting domus for the family of a senior civil servant. A pair of French doors led outdoors from the dining room at the back of the dwelling and, as we stepped outside, I mentioned what an attractive back yard they had. 'Garden,' he corrected me, one of the endless small cultural confusions that bedevil Canadians in Britain. Two words had betrayed my rough postcolonial origins. In his world a garden was a tranquil enclave of lawns and flowers. In mine a garden might be a plot of worthy vegetables or a handsome floral border, but it formed part of something larger and rather more crude – a yard.

The yards of farm homes needn't detain us here. They stood adjacent to the house and formed part of the family's work space, especially that of women. Some farmsteads boasted the close-clipped lawns and lush flower beds that by the late nineteenth century were often thought signs of progressive agricultural practice. But most farms showed no hint of such refinements. Their yards were taken up by kitchen gardens, chicken coops, animal pens, storage sheds, and the like. In any case, the grassy swards and floral bowers found in occasional farmyards did little more than decorate utilitarian spaces.

80. Sir Casimir Gzowski's house, Toronto, 1901.

81. Residence of M.O. Hammond, 148 Albany Avenue, Toronto, c. 1900.

Urban and suburban yards were quite another matter. Over the last two centuries they've passed through a dramatic evolution. As we've seen, the urban home moved about on its lot during these years. It sought to emulate the suburban or country villa, standing alone in a natural setting. The gradual retreat from the front of the lot left a growing expanse of open space soon overtaken by grass, shrubs, and flowers. These formed part of the dwelling's visual presence, proclaiming the taste and social status of its owners to interested passers-by. The handsome gardens in front of the Toronto home of Sir Casimir Gzowski provided a striking frame for the well-proportioned Italianate house owned by one of the city's leading families (Figure 80). In this turn-of-the-century picture, taken by a prominent studio photographer from the city, the house and gardens seem posed for a formal sitting. They stand in sharp contrast to the far more modest residence of M.O. Hammond, whose front garden consisted only of a small plot of close-cropped grass (Figure 81). Intentionally or not, this simple front yard also made a public comment about the Hammonds' claims to status.

From the late nineteenth century on, as the suburban home receded ever farther from the front of the lot, lawns usurped most of the vacant spaces left behind. (Only gardeners recognize the subtle imperialism of plants, in this case the aptly named grass called creeping red fescue.) The result was considerable stretches of clipped green turf occasionally broken by a struggling bush or tree. This condition in cities and suburbs alike long remained a source of despair to the nation's beleaguered landscape architecture profession. According to Frederick Todd, who practised in Montreal during the early twentieth century, it remained the 'rule rather than the exception to see costly private residences and public buildings standing bleak and lonely without a tree or shrub to relieve the hard outline of the architecture.'[106]

Todd would have been just as discouraged by the general appearance of the hundreds of new subdivisions that mushroomed across the country half a century later. Front lawns had few social uses for household members, apart perhaps from children's games. Much too exposed to public view, they seldom invited outdoor leisure. In fact, they had little utility at all for adults – unless we include a sense of oneness with nature that might come from the continual round of fertilizing, mowing, weeding, and raking that was the suburban homeowner's destiny.

The lawn's symbolic value, however, is quite another matter. A recent history of the American lawn points out its central position in the nation's popular culture, a place it has occupied since the lawn became 'democratized' in the early twentieth century.[107] Well-clipped lawns bespeak domesticity, good housekeeping, and a healthy family life inside the home. They also symbolize human control over nature and the ceaseless struggle to preserve this control. The suburban lawn even expresses the neighbourliness and social equality – or perhaps conformity? – that seem to characterize the vast urban housing tracts built by American developers throughout much of the twentieth century. Given the pervasive influence of American mass culture on Canada, we shouldn't be surprised to find these values attached to suburban lawns north of the border too.

The urban back yard passed through its own transformation during the same period. As photographs of the mid-nineteenth century Toronto skyline indicate, back yards in the city's centre had nothing to do with gardening (Figures 62 and 63). Here household-ers built or stored those things they wished kept from public view: woodsheds and privies, stables and chicken coops, clotheslines and garbage. A few resolute souls may have gardened these spaces but green paint was much more visible than green plants in the mid-Victorian city core. Even when lot sizes began to grow after the turn of the century, the spaces behind urban and suburban homes remained crowded with garages and sheds, leaving room for little more than a small vegetable plot and a few blades of grass. The back yards of A.J. Ames and his Ottawa neighbours, glimpsed in a 1910 photograph, could scarcely be considered a gardener's para-dise (Figure 82).

Still, ornamental gardening had long had a following in Canada, in fact from the early years of European settlement. Nineteenth-century villas often featured carefully groomed land-scapes in the French or British manner – the style depending on the owners' cultural origins. One sign of a growing interest in domestic gardening was the founding of local horticultural soci-eties. In 1834, a group of Torontonians established the first one in

82. Back yard of A.J. Ames, Ottawa,
c. 1910.

the colonies; by the early 1900s there were sixty in Ontario alone and numerous others across the country.[108] A gentle (and at least initially a genteel) pastime, gardening grew more popular as the twentieth century progressed, while the increasing size of building lots gave homeowners expanding scope for their horticultural ambitions, especially in the suburbs. Thus in time the back yard metamorphosed into the garden, complete with brave shrubs, bristly lawns, and ambitious flower beds. By the mid-twentieth century gardening had become another feature of middle-class life, even for those on modest incomes.

Figure 83 tells the story well: a small Ottawa bungalow in 1946, set on a spacious suburban lot, with an ample garden space behind the dwelling and floral borders marking the frontiers of neighbouring properties. Dad waters the flowers, Mom rakes the grass, and the kids play happily together on the lawn. The original photograph caption reads 'A Family Works and Relaxes in the Pleasant Garden of Their Home,' an apt summary of the powerful home-centred family values that lay at the heart of postwar domesticity. As we see in this picture, the focus of outdoor household life has shifted to the back of the house, to an attractive naturalistic setting suitable for family activities and well away from the public thoroughfare. The presence of symbolic rather than physical barriers between the lots spoke of a certain commitment to neighbourliness, based on shared assumptions about garden maintenance. Still to come were the hedges and high fences of the more recent past, which have helped turn the back garden into a private family preserve.

We might also pause a moment to consider the relationship between gardens on one hand and gender roles on the other. The British social historians Leonore Davidoff and Catherine Hall have noted that the garden held important, distinctive meanings for men and women of the emerging middle class in early-nineteenth-century England.[109] Not long before, cultivating plants had been far beneath the dignity of anyone claiming membership in polite society. But in the new suburban homes of the burgeoning industrial and commercial middle class, gardening became an acceptable recreation for men and women alike. A businessman might mow his lawn without threatening his social standing. Similarly, his wife could cultivate plants on her own – though the situation she faced

83. A family works and relaxes in the pleasant garden of their home, Community Chest Drive, Ottawa, September 1946.

was somewhat more complex because garden work was associated with manual labour, to say nothing of dirt and manure. Increasingly middle-class women found an acceptable outlet for their agrarian passions in flower gardening, avoiding the more practical – and compromising – herbs and vegetables. By the end of the nineteenth century, gardening had become an accepted pastime for upper- and middle-class women throughout the English-speaking world, an extension of their domestic roles into the world beyond the kitchen door. Some have even suggested that the path to women's empowerment passed through the garden.[110]

4 | Privacy and the Canadian Home

Looking back such a distance in time it's difficult to fathom what privacy might have meant to most of our ancestors: to the eighteenth-century habitant in a one-room dwelling beside the St Lawrence River; to the nineteenth-century Upper Canadian pioneer in a small home on Lake Ontario; to the preindustrial artisan who laboured and lived in a little house on a narrow street in a busy colonial town. What we now consider the foundation of personal privacy, the opportunity to be alone, must have been almost unimaginable to many of our forbears. A fortunate minority, more wealthy, often more literate, and therefore better known to us today, possessed somewhat larger homes. But often their families were large as well. If by privacy we mean personal seclusion, it must surely have been uncommon even among the upper middle class in early Canada. To be sure it was available outdoors, in the woods and fields and forests. But indoor spaces were shared spaces; whatever moments people passed at home alone had to be snatched when opportunity presented them. This fact was doubly true during the long cold months of winter, when hard weather often discouraged people from venturing out of doors.

Family or household privacy also took quite different forms then than it does today. A home, of course, was its residents' space, the place where they ate and slept, worked and played, loved and argued. But as historians of the family have long known, these homes often harboured more than the nuclear family. Kin, boarders, and servants commonly formed part of the household as well, at least at some point in family life's long cycle. The boundaries of the household were once more porous than they've become, and all those who regularly slept under one roof could claim some rights of membership in the group. Those rights might be broad or narrow depending on one's relationship to the head of the house. As we've observed, the Woolseys' male servants sometimes had to sleep in the kitchen. But they remained household members no matter how menial their lot.

More open forms of sociability also characterized the early colonial household. As eighteenth- and nineteenth-century diaries and letters tell us, friends and families visited regularly in one another's homes, sometimes invited, often dropping by unannounced, to spend a convivial evening or a Sunday afternoon. We might reasonably assume that they acknowledged the boundary of private household space by knocking before entering. But that boundary might mean relatively little because refusing hospitality to a friend on a casual visit could cause grave offence. It may be that towns like Calvert – where friends even drop in between courses of a meal without so much as a tap on the door – still follow social practices once widespread.

Since those times we've seen a transformation in personal and family privacy, centred on the home. While privacy is something rather difficult to quantify it's obvious that we now have much more of it than our ancestors could have imagined. Middle-class dwellings now have spaces we can claim for ourselves: my bedroom, my corner, my study. Meanwhile our homes stand ever more aloof from outsiders: kin, friends, and strangers alike, even in densely built cities. They, too, are much more private places than Canadian dwellings once were.

In the early colonial years only the wealthy knew something of personal privacy in its modern forms, and even then only in small degree. But as the homes of less privileged families began to grow and their interiors to subdivide, the domestic boundaries between self and others began to sharpen. During the early and middle years of the nineteenth century in a growing proportion of Canadian homes, the number of rooms began to multiply and to serve more specific purposes. Married couples were probably first to benefit as they claimed private sleeping quarters for themselves. But in time most other household members gained new access to personal space – even servants. The modern notion of a room of one's own developed later still, at a point where the rising trend in rooms per dwelling intersected with the falling one of family size. Before then even the privileged adolescents of the rich normally shared bedrooms with their siblings, unless they were the only ones of their sex in the family. The equation of one child with one room didn't have much currency until after the First World War, by which time the falling birth rate had reduced family size dramatically. The baby boom after the Second World War didn't deflect the trend. By this time the small home was on the wane in Canada, and average household size continued to fall despite the surge in births.

The changing technologies of domestic life also left their mark on this evolving sense of personal privacy. In time, newer, less costly forms of heating and lighting allowed family members to remove themselves from one another's company at home whenever they wished. No longer bound by the need to share a single source of heat or light, they could retire alone to a quiet corner as they desired. In a northern country such as Canada, these were particularly important innovations. Meanwhile the several gifts of the nineteenth-century porcelain revolution – flush toilets, bathroom sinks, bathtubs, hot and cold running water – transformed the hygienic customs of a people newly sensitive to the social meanings of odours, those of their own bodies in particular. The new taboo of the objectionable self encouraged this flowering sense of personal privacy, nowhere more so than within the home.

It would be wrong, however, to think of these developments as simply a vast, continuous, and uniform evolution in the home lives of all Canadians. Quite the contrary, the many forms of personal privacy have evolved in various ways, touching individuals and social groups quite differently according to time, place, and circumstance. Generally speaking they spread from the wealthy and well-to-do to the general population. Those at the top of the economic heap have always been able to buy the greater access to privacy linked with large homes and new technologies before anyone else could afford them. Similarly, the poor at any time have tended to live in much smaller, less technologically advanced dwellings. In fact, as the broad trend has been toward ever greater privacy for ever greater numbers, its lack has come to be one of poverty's leading features.

The path of diffusion has also led from large cities to small towns and then to the countryside. Wealthy city residents introduced the first privacy-enhancing technologies to their homes, and in time these innovations spread widely in their communities. Small-town and rural householders generally lagged well behind. The cost of building new infrastructures was high in thinly settled areas and so it was expensive to link individual homes with new systems. Still, city life conferred disadvantages too. Higher land and building costs constrained the size of urban homes, as well as the yards surrounding them, particularly in the nineteenth century but also in the more recent past. Conversely, large houses abounded throughout suburban, small-town, and rural Canada from the early nineteenth century on, offering their residents the prospect of more chances for personal seclusion than all but the most favoured city dwellers.

The growth of privacy was also related to the settlement experience. As a European settler society, Canada absorbed wave upon wave of newcomers from the seventeenth century onward. Until the First World War many, probably most, settled in rural places. While by no means poor – even assisted migration was costly – these men and women often had few funds at their disposal, and they prudently tended to invest in their well-being before their comfort. Thus the small pioneer cabin. In time and with some measure of economic success, large homes replaced small ones, expanding the space available to the family. While a common experience on all settler frontiers, this feature of Canada's housing history was particularly visible during the settlement years in the prairie West, where newcomers often deferred their comfort and privacy in return for a fresh start in life. I suspect that the same progression from small house to large was also part of the urban immigrant experience, though we'll never know how common it was. It certainly formed part of the myth of new world upward mobility, a dream that has long fuelled the aspirations of so many new arrivals.

A word about gender seems appropriate at this point. One theme in recent writing about the history of the house has emphasized the division of homes according to sex – female space and male space – depending on who held authority or responsibility in any one part of the dwelling. (The kitchen was female space, the workshop male space, and so forth.) Some feminist critics have further argued that nineteenth- and twentieth-century housing design has often reflected, indeed reinforced, the subordination of women by creating superior and inferior zones, and then assigning the latter to women. Unfortunately, however, the analysts aren't of one mind on these issues. Occasionally they even disagree about which rooms belonged to each sex. Pocius suggests, quite persuasively I think, that the entire house is generally seen as a woman's responsibility and thus is her place, even when men are present.[111]

In fact, gender categories don't shed much light on the relations between privacy and domesticity. With the possible exception of the kitchen, there never have been parts of the Canadian dwelling that one sex could claim as its own, unlike pre-revolutionary China, for example, where women have long had domestic spaces reserved to them.[112] In Canada women and men have always shared all parts of the house, no matter whose space it might seem to be. Even the most intimate acts occur in rooms that both sexes use, though the doors are normally closed to respect the occupants' modesty.

Children were late to know the changes that transformed household space. Yet in some respects their lives altered more dramatically than any other family members as a result of them. Only since the mid-twentieth century, and the advent of the small family, have they been able to claim their own private space more or less by right. Presently one child, one bedroom is the norm in all but the poorest families and, like proud householders everywhere, children furnish and decorate their spaces to suit their own tastes – their home within a home.

Turning to the evolution of family or household privacy, again we see complex patterns of change instead of a simple straight-line trend. The rural experience has varied greatly across time and geographic space. The St Lawrence Valley communities of the mid-eighteenth century and the ranching communities of western Canada more than a century later represent extremes of cohesion and dispersion. Both settings assured a measure of household privacy, but in ranch country privacy shaded into isolation. When compared with Quebec, the greater separation of farm homes from public spaces throughout most of English Canada speaks of a greater distance between the family and the community, particularly in the prairie West. These social distances grew greater still with the ongoing depopulation of rural areas in central Canada during the late nineteenth and early twentieth centuries, and also in the West in the more recent past.

Urban and suburban dwellings reached the peak of their seclusion during the early twentieth century, when the villa ideal of the freestanding family home reached the height of its popularity. And even though its lustre has dimmed since then, the freestanding house remains the preference of most Canadians today. What have changed over the years are its orientation and use of outdoor settings. The suburban home once turned its face to the public, to the roads and walkways that tied it to its community. It invoked a neighbourly sociability through porches, verandahs, and front garden displays – effective in Canada during the warmer seasons at least. But in the 1960s and '70s it turned its back on public spaces, more and more preoccupied with enhancing the family's privacy. The result is that the social life of transitional spaces between the home and the road or sidewalk has eroded almost everywhere in Canada, the suburbs especially . Householders have turned instead to their decks, their patios, and their barbecues – to a domestic ideal focused on the home's interior and garden.

Yet even during the early twentieth century, when the detached suburban dwelling stood at the height of its popularity, other common house forms drew people closer together. Row houses in Ontario, 'plexes' in Quebec, and apartment buildings in the nation's larger cities created far more densely populated housing than provided by the single-family garden home, and over time their numbers have grown dramatically. These examples contradict the proposition that as the distances between people and between dwellings have grown privacy has increased too. The relationship between privacy and the amount of available domestic space is not a straightforward one. Over the past century or so, those living in multifamily buildings have known their own forms of domestic privacy, even while living closely together.

The modern highrise apartment, for example, has a high population density, yet those of us who have lived in them know what deeply private places they can be. It's not merely possible but common to live in a downtown tower and know almost nothing of the folks who live next door – on the other side of a ten-centimetre concrete wall. In this case propinquity defines the distance between neighbours, who live 'alone together' – in the luminous phrase of the American apartment's leading historian.[113] To know the same isolation you'd have to live in the depths of the wilderness. In twentieth-century Canada growing privacy and rising urban density have walked hand in hand. It seems likely that the relationship between them is causal, that living ever more closely together has prompted apartment dwellers to defend their private spaces with ever more vigilance. Their norms and customs promote respectful neighbourly distance much more than familiarity.

At the same time, high-density dwellings provide a somewhat qualified privacy, though we've no way of knowing if their residents feel any less private than those who live in garden homes. What they lack most of all are the spatial buffers provided by front lawns and side yards, the transitional zones that mingle the public and the private under community scrutiny. Domestic privacy in apartment buildings is kept indoors and even there it has limits. The sounds and smells of daily life easily travel the short distances involved. A burnt dinner or a marital quarrel can be difficult to conceal. These dwellings now seem the homes of the future in our larger cities. If so, privacy as our parents and grandparents knew it in small-town and small-city Canada may become a thing of the past or, at least, a thing of the suburbs.

Twentieth-century communications technologies have also reshaped household and personal privacy at a time when the amount of interior domestic space available to most people has grown. Over time the telephone, the radio, and television, and lately the fax and the Internet, have brought the community into the heart of the home, bypassing the front door in the process. Each innovation has strengthened the links formed by its predecessors, binding the inner sanctum of the modern house ever more tightly to the wide wide world. For some time now it's been possible to be alone at home and still be anything but private, and the range of these possibilities has broadened greatly over the past half century. In various ways we now can enjoy the society of others while remaining at home by ourselves. The full implications of this revolution for personal and household privacy are far from clear at this writing. We tend to view them in contradictory ways: as worrisome challenges to our privacy at home, as welcome increases in the range of choices before us. In time, presumably, they'll reshape the notion and experience of domestic privacy once more, just as new technologies have done in the past.

And finally a moment of speculation about a closely related matter. The growth of individualism has long been one of the leading features of Western societies, Canada among them. Over time a powerful sense of the uniqueness of the self, its independence from the social group, and the value of its independent thought and action have become defining characteristics of Western modernity. Some historians have found Western individualism deeply embedded in the mediaeval past. Others see capitalism and political liberalism as seedbeds of these convictions. That acutely perceptive French observer Alexis de Tocqueville, noting the force of individualism in early-nineteenth-century America, located its centre in the individual's 'circle of family and friends.'

We probably should add the family home to his list. The folklorist Henry Glassie, for one, rightly points to the great psychic power of the house and its spaces. From the late eighteenth century onward, the evolving shape of the family and that of the domestic spaces it occupied promoted the growth of both household and personal privacy. At various times and to a greater or lesser degree, this process unfolded in Canada and the many other 'overseas Europes' as much as in northwestern Europe itself. Though it has taken many forms, known retreats as well as advances, touched lives in many different ways, privacy is something we have now all come to expect for ourselves and our families. Privacy from strangers, privacy from kin; privacy to seek our goals, privacy to be ourselves. The link between the history of individuality and the history of the dwelling is nebulous but nonetheless real. The roots of Canadian individualism are no doubt many stranded. But some of them lie in the history of the nation's homes and gardens, settings that fostered a sense of the private and independent self.

Notes

AO   Archives of Ontario, Toronto, Ontario
CRA   City of Richmond Archives, Richmond, British Columbia
CTA   City of Toronto Archives, Toronto, Ontario
Glenbow   Glenbow Archives, Calgary, Alberta
McCord   McCord Museum of Canadian History, Montreal, Quebec
MUL   McGill University Library, Montreal, Quebec
NAC   National Archives of Canada, Ottawa, Ontario
NGC   National Gallery of Canada, Ottawa, Ontario
NSA   Archives and Record Management, Nova Scotia,
            Halifax, Nova Scotia
PAA   Provincial Archives of Alberta, Edmonton, Alberta
ROM   Royal Ontario Museum, Toronto, Ontario
VPL   Special Collections, Vancouver Public Library,
            Vancouver, British Columbia

1 Thomas A. Markus, *Buildings & Power: Freedom and Control in the Origin of Modern Building Types* (London and New York: Routledge, 1993), 27.
2 R. Cole Harris, ed., *Historical Atlas of Canada*, vol. 1, *From the Beginning to 1800* (Toronto: University of Toronto Press, 1987), plate 55; Michel Lessard et Gilles Vilandré, *La maison traditionelle au Québec* (Montreal: Les Éditions de l'homme, 1974), 228; Susanne Jean, 'La maison rurale de l'Ile d'Orléans: Aménagement de l'espace intérieur entre 1761 et 1767,' in *Habitation rurale au Québec*, ed. Jean-Claude Dupont (Montreal: Cahiers du Québec, Hurtubise HMH, 1978), 13-28.
3 Harold Kalman, *A History of Canadian Architecture*, vol. 1 (Toronto: Oxford University Press, 1994), 85.
4 Joann Latremouille, *Pride of Home: The Working-Class Housing Tradition in Nova Scotia, 1749-1949* (Hantsport, NS: Lancelot Press, 1986), 17; David B. Mills, 'The Development of Folk Architecture in Trinity Bay, Newfoundland,' in *The Peopling of Newfoundland: Essays in Historical Geography*, ed. John J. Mannion, Social and Economic Papers no. 8 (St John's, NF: St John's Institute of Social and Economic Research, Memorial University, 1977), 77-101.
5 D.C. Tibbetts, 'The Newfoundland Tilt,' *Habitat* 11, 5 (1968): 14-7.
6 John Howison, *Sketches of Upper Canada, Domestic, Local, and Characteristic: To Which Are Added, Practical Details for the Information of Emigrants*

of Every Class; and Some Recollections of the United States of America (Edinburgh: Oliver and Boyd, 1821), 20, 247, and 252.

7 Donald G. Wetherell and Irene R.A. Kmet, *Homes in Alberta: Building, Trends, and Design, 1870-1967* (Edmonton: University of Alberta Press, 1991), 3-41; John Lehr, *Ukrainian Vernacular Architecture in Alberta* (Edmonton: Alberta Culture, Historical Resources Division, 1976); Canada, *Census of Canada*, 1911.

8 Jean-Pierre Hardy, 'Niveaux de richesse et intérieurs domestiques dans le quartier Saint-Roch à Québec, 1820-1850,' *Material History Bulletin* 17 (1983): 73; Hélène Bourque, *La maison de faubourg: L'architecture domestique des faubourgs Saint-Jean et Saint-Roch avant 1845* (Quebec: Institut québécois de recherche sur la culture, 1991), 98-9.

9 Jason Gilliland and Sherry Olson, 'Claims on Housing Space in Nineteenth-Century Montreal,' *Urban History Review* 26, 2 (1998): 4; for Quebec village housing see Gilles Lauzon, 'Habitat ouvrier et révolution industrielle: Le cas du village St-Augustin' (MA thesis, Université du Québec à Montréal, 1986), 166; Réal Bélanger, George S. Mooney, and Pierre Boucher, *Les vieux logements de Montréal* (Montreal: Commission métropolitaine de Montréal, Département d'urbanisation et de recherche, 1938), 10; for overcrowding rates in English Canada see Jill Wade, *Houses for All: The Struggle for Social Housing in Vancouver, 1919-50* (Vancouver: UBC Press, 1994), 56.

10 Heather MacDougall, *Activists and Advocates: Toronto's Health Department, 1883-1983* (Toronto: Dundurn Press, 1990), 78-9; Guy Groux and Catherine Lévy, *La possession ouvrière: Du taudis à la propriété (xixe-xxe siècle)* (Paris: Les Éditions de l'Atelier, 1993), 19; T.C. Smout, *A History of the Scottish People, 1830-1950* (London: Collins, 1986), 33-5.

11 Dimensions of Dwelling Houses, 1795-1852, Woolsey Family Papers, MG24 D1, vol. 1, file 2, 603-4, NAC.

12 France Gagnon-Pratte, *L'Architecture et la nature à Québec au dix-neuvième siècle. Les villas* (Quebec: Ministère des Affaires culturelles, 1980); for information about the Plamondon house see Yves Laframboise, *Neuville: Architecture traditionelle* (Quebec: Ministère des Affaires culturelles du Québec, 1976), 207-17.

13 Allan Penney, *The Simeon Perkins House: An Architectural Interpretation 1767-1987*, Curatorial report no. 60 (Halifax: Nova Scotia Museum, 1987), 96-146.

14 Ibid.; Arthur W. Wallace, *An Album of Drawings of Early Buildings in Nova Scotia* (Halifax: Heritage Trust of Nova Scotia, 1976); Nathalie Clerk, *Prescott House, Starrs Point, Nova Scotia* (Ottawa: Parks Canada, 1987); Lessard and Vilandré, *La maison traditionelle au Québec*, 228-33; Peter Moogk, 'At Home in Early Niagara Township,' *The Capital Years: Niagara-on-the Lake, 1792-1796*, ed. Richard Merritt, Nancy Butler, and Michael Power (Toronto and Oxford: Dundurn Press, 1991), 165-85; Peter Ennals and Deryck Holdsworth, 'Vernacular Architecture and the Cultural Landscape of the Maritime Provinces – A Reconnaissance,' *Acadiensis* 10, 2 (1981): 86-106.

15 Herbert Brown Ames, *The City below the Hill*, 2nd ed. (Toronto: University of Toronto Press, 1972), 61-5; Bettina Bradbury, *Working Families: Age, Gen-*

der, and Daily Survival in Industrializing Montreal (Toronto: McClelland and Stewart, 1993), 77-8; for Hamilton see Michael Doucet and John Weaver, *Housing the North American City* (Montreal and Kingston: McGill-Queen's University Press, 1991), 435-9.

16 Manuscript Census of Canada, 1891, The Territories, Alberta, A14, page 9, family 43.

17 Michael Piva, *The Condition of the Working Class in Toronto – 1900-1921* (Ottawa: University of Ottawa Press, 1979), 130; Wade, *Houses for All*, 56.

18 John Lambert, *Travels through Canada and the United States of North America, in the Years 1806, 1807, & 1808* (London: Cradock and Joy, 1813), 152-3.

19 Lessard and Vilandré, *La maison traditionelle au Québec*, 230-3; Christian Dessureault, John A. Dickinson, and Thomas Wien, 'Living Standards of Norman and Canadian Peasants 1690-1835,' in *Material Culture: Consumption, Life-style, Standard of Living, 1500-1900*, ed. Anton J. Schuurman and Lorena S. Walsh, Proceedings of the Eleventh International Economic History Conference, Milan, 1994 (Milan: Università Bocconi, 1994), 95-112.

20 Wallace, *An Album of Drawings*, 47-9.

21 M.J. Daunton, *House and Home in the Victorian City: Working-Class Housing, 1850-1914* (London: Edward Arnold, 1983); Stefan Muthesius, *The English Terraced House* (New Haven and London: Yale University Press, 1982); David B. Hanna, 'The Creation of an Early Victorian Suburb in Montreal,' in *Cities and Urbanization: Canadian Historical Perspectives*, ed. Gilbert A. Stelter (Toronto: Copp Clark Pitman, 1990), 39-65; Margaret Angus, *The Old Stones of Kingston: Its Buildings before 1867* (Toronto: University of Toronto Press, 1966), 28, 84.

22 David B. Hanna, 'The Layered City: A Revolution in Housing in Mid-Nineteenth Century Montreal,' *Shared Spaces/Partage de l'espace*, McGill University, Department of Geography, Occasional paper no. 6 (1986); Lauzon, 'Habitat ouvrier et révolution industrielle'; Bélanger, Mooney, and Boucher, *Vieux logements*.

23 Jean-Claude Marsan, *Montreal in Evolution* (Montreal and Kingston: McGill-Queen's University Press, 1981), 265-81.

24 Vincent J. Scully, *The Shingle Style and the Stick Style: Architectural Theory and Design from Richardson to the Origins of Wright*, rev. ed. (New Haven and London: Yale University Press, 1971).

25 Wetherell and Kmet, *Homes in Alberta*, 68-9.

26 Anthony D. King, *The Bungalow: The Production of a Global Culture*, 2nd ed. (New York, Oxford: Oxford University Press, 1995), 127-55.

27 Wetherell and Kmet, *Homes in Alberta*, 74; Deryck Holdsworth, 'Regional Distinctiveness in an Industrial Age: Some California Influences on British Columbia Housing,' *The American Review of Canadian Studies* 12, 2 (1982): 64-81.

28 For heating technology of the era see Georges Gauthier-Larouche, 'Evolution de la maison rurale traditionelle dans la région de Québec (Étude Ethnographique),' in *Les Archives de Folklore*, vol. 15 (Quebec: Les presses de l'université Laval, 1974), 142-4. For the impressions of English travellers see Howison, *Sketches of Upper Canada*, 209; Lambert, *Travels through*

Canada, 314-7; William S. Moorsom, *Letters from Nova Scotia* (London: Colburn and Bentley, 1830), 305. Quotation from Alexander Peter Hanley, interview, 25 February 1972, phonotape, acc.71.6, PAA.

29 Alan Gowans, *The Comfortable House: North American Suburban Architecture, 1890-1930* (Cambridge, MA: MIT Press, 1986), 27.

30 The Montreal survey is contained in Bélanger, Mooney, and Boucher, *Vieux logements*, 11. The earlier Toronto survey is *Report of the Lieutenant-Governor's Committee on Housing Conditions in Toronto* (Toronto: Hunter-Rose, 1934), 129-31, 136-8. See also John R. Miron, *Housing in Postwar Canada: Demographic Change, Household Formation, and Housing Demand* (Montreal and Kingston: McGill-Queen's University Press, 1988), 184; Statistics Canada, *Household Facilities and Equipment*, Catalogue no. 64-202 (Ottawa: Statistics Canada, 1991), 16.

31 Jacques Bernier, *Les intérieurs domestiques des menuisiers et charpentiers de la région de Québec, 1810-1819* (Ottawa: Musées nationaux du Canada, 1977), 49; Loris S. Russell, *A Heritage of Light: Lamps and Lighting in the Early Canadian Home* (Toronto: University of Toronto Press, 1968); Margaret Howard Blom and Thomas E. Blom, eds., *Canada Home: Juliana Horatia Ewing's Fredericton Letters, 1867-1869* (Vancouver: University of British Columbia Press, 1983), 111; 'The Price of Light,' *The Economist*, 22-8 October 1994, 84.

32 Bélanger, Mooney, and Boucher, *Vieux logements*, 11; *Report of the Lieutenant-Governor's Committee*, 129-31.

33 Alison Prentice, Paula Borne, Gail Cuthbert Brandt, Wendy Mitchinson, and Naomi Black, *Canadian Women: A History* (Toronto: Harcourt Brace Jovanovich, 1988), 245.

34 Robert Laroque, dit de Roquebrune, *Testament de mon enfance. Récit* (Paris: Plon, 1951), 64.

35 Albert Eide Parr, 'Heating, Lighting, Plumbing, and Human Relations,' *Landscape* 19, 1 (1970): 28-9.

36 Roquebrune, *Testament*, 14-5.

37 Maureen Ogle, *All the Modern Conveniences: American Household Plumbing, 1840-1890* (Baltimore: Johns Hopkins University Press, 1996), 36-8.

38 Roy Palmer, *The Water Closet: A New History* (Newton Abbott: David and Charles, 1973), 22-4, 92-4; Lawrence Wright, *Clean and Decent; the fascinating history of the bathroom and the water closet, and of sundry habits, fashions and accessories of the toilet, principally in Great Britain, France, and America* (Toronto: University of Toronto Press, 1967), 201-5.

39 Letty Anderson, 'Water-Supply,' in *Building Canada: A History of Public Works*, ed. Norman R. Ball (Toronto: University of Toronto Press, 1988), 195-220; Douglas Baldwin, 'Sewerage,' in *Building Canada*, ed. Ball, 221-44; Catherine Brace, 'One Hundred and Twenty Years of Sewerage: The Provision of Sewers in Toronto 1793-1913' (MA thesis, Department of Geography, University of Toronto, 1993), 44-7, 69-70.

40 Scott Home, plan view, 1878, Horwood Collection, C11-150-0-1(158)1, AO, and Sketch of Proposed House for Geo. Dickson, Esq., 1880, C11-168-0-1(174)1, AO.

41 Brace, 'One Hundred and Twenty Years of Sewerage,' 120, 160-1; Bélanger, Mooney, and Boucher, *Vieux logements*, 11-2; *Report of the Lieutenant-Governor's Committee*, 129-31, 136-8; Wade, *Houses for All*, 56.

42 Miron, *Housing in Postwar Canada*, 187.

43 Norbert Elias, *The History of Manners: The Civilizing Process*, vol. 1 (New York: Pantheon, 1982), 129-43.

44 Margaret W. Andrews, 'Sanitary Conveniences and the Retreat of the Frontier, Vancouver, 1886-1929,' *BC Studies* 87 (Autumn 1990): 3-22.

45 Alain Corbin, *The Foul and the Fragrant: Odor and the French Social Imagination* (Cambridge, MA: Harvard University Press, 1986), especially 161-75. See also P.R. Gleichmann, 'Des villes propres et sans odeur. La vidange du corps humain: équipments et domestication,' *Urbi* (April 1982): 88-100.

46 M. Farley, O. Keel, and C. Limoges, 'Les commencements de l'administration montréalaise de la santé publique (1865-1885),' *Journal of the History of Canadian Science, Technology and Medicine* 20 (1982): 26.

47 City of Toronto, *By-laws*, 1877, By-law 782, and 1878, By-law 840; City of Montreal, *By-laws of the City of Montreal*, 1931, By-law 197, 1891.

48 The Hanley interview refers to the location of outhouses for women and men. For the location of indoor toilets, see also W.B. Robinson Residence, Richmond Street East, Toronto, 1856, C11-97-0-1(106)3, AO; Haggarty Home, 1852, C11-76-0-1(81)4, AO.

49 John Kenneth Galbraith, *The Scotch* (New York: New American Library, 1964), 15; Hanley interview.

50 Monique Eleb-Vidal with Ann Debarre-Blanchard. *Architectures de la vie privée: Maisons et mentalités xviie-xixe siècles* (Brussels: Archives d'architecture moderne, 1989), 206; Jean-Pierre Goubert, *The Conquest of Water: The Advent of Health in the Industrial Age* (Princeton, NJ: Princeton University Press, 1989), 242.

51 Paul Labonne and Jean-François Leclerc, *Prendre son bain aux bains: L'histoire des bains publics de Montréal (1860-1960) / Time for a Scrub: The History of Montreal's Public Baths (1860-1960)* (Montreal: n.p., 1996).

52 'Baths for Women,' *Herald* (Montreal), 31 July 1897.

53 Bélanger, Mooney, and Boucher, *Vieux logements*, 11; *Report of the Lieutenant-Governor's Committee*, 129-31, 136-8; Miron, *Housing in Postwar Canada*, 187; Statistics Canada, *Household Facilities and Equipment*, 1996, 45.

54 Paul-Louis Martin, 'Le discours de l'habitation, la maison rurale comme indicateur de changement culturel,' Conférence prononcée dans le cadre du séminaire 'Espace et culture' (Dir. Robert Muchembled), Université de Paris-Nord XIII, April 1994, 66; John J. Mannion, *Irish Settlements in Eastern Canada: A Study of Cultural Transfer and Adaptation* (Toronto: University of Toronto Press for the University of Toronto Department of Geography, 1974), 151-63; Wetherell and Kmet, *Homes in Alberta*, 25-7.

55 George Stephen Jones, *A Love Story from 19th Century Quebec: The Diary of George Stephen Jones*, ed. W. Peter Ward (Peterborough, ON: Broadview Press, 1989).

56 Daunton, *House and Home*, 277-81; for an American example of the rural-urban contrast see Sally McMurry, 'City Parlor, Country Sitting Room: Rural

Vernacular Design and the American Parlor, 1840-1900,' *Winterthur Portfolio* 20, 4 (1985): 261-80.

57 Arthur Loesser, *Men, Women and Pianos: A Social History* (New York: Simon and Schuster, 1954).

58 Mary O'Brien, *The Journals of Mary O'Brien, 1828-1838,* ed. Audrey Saunders Miller (Toronto: Macmillan, 1968), 17.

59 Statistics Canada, *Household Facilities and Equipment,* 1953, 17; and 1960, 20.

60 Lessard and Vilandré, *La maison traditionelle au Québec,* 228-33.

61 Mannion, *Irish Settlements in Eastern Canada,* 158.

62 Gerald L. Pocius, *A Place to Belong: Community Order and Everyday Space in Calvert, Newfoundland* (Montreal and Kingston: McGill-Queen's University Press, 1991), 221, 228-32.

63 Wetherell and Kmet, *Homes in Alberta,* 74.

64 Elizabeth C. Cromley, 'Transforming the Food Axis: Houses, Tools, Modes of Analysis,' *Material History Review* 44 (Fall 1996): 18-9.

65 Hale quoted in Kalman, *History of Canadian Architecture,* 85; Lessard and Vilandré, *La maison traditionelle au Québec,* 229.

66 Bernier, *Les intérieurs domestiques,* 65-7; Hardy, 'Niveaux de richesse et intérieurs domestiques'; Lambert, *Travels through Canada,* 152-3.

67 Louisa Collins, *Louisa's Diary: The Journal of a Farmer's Daughter, Dartmouth, 1815,* ed. Dale McClare (Halifax: Nova Scotia Museum, 1989), 21.

68 Bernier, *Les intérieurs domestiques,* 63-4; Annmarie Adams and Peter Gossage, '*Chez Fadette:* Girlhood, Family, and Private Space in Late Nineteenth-Century Saint-Hyacinthe,' *Urban History Review* 26, 2 (1998): 56-68; Eleb-Vidal and Debarre-Blanchard, *Architectures de la vie privée,* 218-9.

69 Bélanger, Mooney, and Boucher, *Vieux logements,* 6; Pocius, *A Place to Belong,* 250.

70 Pocius, *A Place to Belong,* 180; see also 221, 250.

71 Canada, *Census of Canada,* 1921, 3: 26, 39; Miron, *Housing in Postwar Canada,* 156; Statistics Canada, 'Occupied Private Dwellings,' *1991 Census of Canada,* Catalogue 93-314 (Ottawa: Industry, Science and Technology Canada, 1993), table 2.

72 François Rémillard and Brian Merrett, *Montreal Architecture: Guide to Styles and Buildings* (Montreal: Meridian Press, 1990), 107, 112; Doucet and Weaver, *Housing the North American City,* 389, 396-7; Richard Dennis, 'Apartment Housing in Canadian Cities, 1900-1940,' *Urban History Review* 26, 2 (1998): 17-31.

73 Miron, *Housing in Postwar Canada,* 156.

74 Harris, *Historical Atlas,* vol. 1, plate 55.

75 For houses built along a shore, see 'A plan of lands, granted to the late Royal Nova Scotia Volunteers at Antigonish on the south side of Cape St Louis, Nova Scotia, 1787' (1914), NMC19511, NAC. For the variety of placements on the Halifax-Windsor route, see Joan Dawson, 'A Glimpse of the "Great Roads" of Nova Scotia in the Early Nineteenth Century,' *The Occasional* 15, 2 (1993): 18, 21.

76 Elizabeth P. Simcoe, 'Mrs. Tice's Farm on the Mountain near Queenston,' 1795, C13922, NAC; O'Brien (née Gapper), *Journals of Mary O'Brien,* 21.

77 George Woodcock and Ivan Avakumovic, *The Doukhobors* (Toronto: Oxford University Press, 1968), 208-24.

78 Wetherell and Kmet, *Homes in Alberta*, 94.

79 Moira O'Neill, 'A Lady's Life on a Ranche,' *Blackwood's Edinburgh Magazine* 163 (January 1898): 2.

80 James S. Ackerman, *The Villa: Form and Ideology of Country Houses*, The A.W. Mellon Lectures in the Fine Arts, 1985, Bollingen Series 35 (Princeton, NJ: Princeton University Press, 1990), 12.

81 Howison, *Sketches of Upper Canada*, 6.

82 P. Bender, *Old and New Canada, 1753-1844* (Montreal: Dawson Brothers, 1882), 185-8.

83 Gagnon-Pratte, *L'Architecture et la nature;* Wallace, *An Album of Drawings*, 39-43.

84 John Maulson, *Park Lots for Suburban Gardens and Villa Residences, Balmoral Avenue, Weston*, no. 90163 (Toronto: Canadian Institute for Historical Microreproductions, 1856), 4.

85 France Gagnon-Pratte, *Country Houses for Montrealers, 1892-1924: The Architecture of E. and W.S. Maxwell* (Montreal: Meridian Press, 1987).

86 For the deeper setback, see, for example, the plans of a large duplex designed in 1878 for W. Scott and built on Dunn Avenue in Toronto. The building was set back thirty feet (nine metres) from the street line (Horwood Collection, C11-150-0-1 [158] 1, AO). For more on multistorey row housing, see Marsan, *Montreal in Evolution*, 265-6; Hanna, 'Creation of an Early Victorian Suburb.'

87 Hélène Desnoyers, 'Le logement ouvrier à Trois-Rivières; l'exemple du secteur Hertel' (PhD diss., Université du Québec à Trois-Rivières, 1988), 28-9; Hanna, 'Creation of an Early Victorian Suburb'; Réjean Legault, 'Architecture et forme urbaine: L'exemple du triplex à Montréal de 1870 à 1914,' *Urban History Review* 18, 1 (1989): 1-10.

88 Thomas Adams, 'The Planning of the New Halifax,' *The Contract Record* (28 August 1918): 680-3; Suzanne Morton, *Ideal Surroundings: Domestic Life in a Working-class Suburb in the 1920s* (Toronto: University of Toronto Press, 1995), 17-22; Carleton University History Collaborative, *Urban and Community Development in Atlantic Canada, 1867-1991*, Canadian Museum of Civilization, History Division, Mercury Series Paper 44 (Hull, QC: Canadian Museum of Civilization, 1993), 79.

89 Pocius, *A Place to Belong*, 155; J.B. Brebner, *The Neutral Yankees of Nova Scotia* (Toronto: McClelland and Stewart, 1969), 151.

90 Doucet and Weaver, *Housing the North American City*, 24-34.

91 Spiro Kostof, *The City Shaped: Urban Patterns and Meanings through History* (Boston: Little, Brown, 1991), 95-157; Harris, *Historical Atlas*, vol. 1, plates 49, 50.

92 Kostof, *City Shaped*, 75-80.

93 Hanna, 'The Layered City.'

94 Wetherell and Kmet, *Homes in Alberta*, 53-4.

95 In 1921, for example, 48.5 percent of all Quebec dwellings were detached compared to 78.9 percent in the rest of Canada. By 1991, the proportion in

Quebec had fallen slightly to 44.6 percent and elsewhere much more dramatically to 61.5 percent. Calculated from Canada, *Census of Canada*, 1921, 3: 26, and Statistics Canada, 'Occupied Private Dwellings,' table 2.

96 In order of size: Toronto, 44.5 percent; Montreal, 29.8 percent; Vancouver, 49.6 percent; Ottawa/Hull, 44.1 percent; Edmonton, 57.4 percent; Calgary, 57.1 percent; Quebec City, 41.7 percent; Winnipeg, 60.7 percent; Hamilton, 59.8 percent; London, 54.8 percent. Calculated from Statistics Canada, 'Occupied Private Dwellings,' table 2.

97 Barrie B. Greenbie, *Spaces: Dimensions of the Human Landscape* (New Haven: Yale University Press, 1981), 6-7.

98 Kent C. Bloomer and Charles W. Moore, *Body, Memory and Architecture* (New Haven and London: Yale University Press, 1977), 1-3.

99 Yi-Fu Tuan, *Segmented Worlds and Self: Group Life and Individual Consciousness* (Minneapolis: University of Minnesota Press, 1982), 83-4.

100 L.G. Thomas, 'Ranch Houses of the Alberta Foothills,' Canadian Historic Sites, *Occasional Papers in Archaeology and History*, No. 20 (Ottawa: Parks Canada, National Historic Parks and Sites Branch, 1979), 139.

101 Pocius, *A Place to Belong*, 173.

102 Annmarie Adams, 'The Eichler Home: Intention and Experience in Postwar Suburbia,' in *Gender, Class, and Shelter: Perspectives in Vernacular Architecture*, vol. 5, ed. Elizabeth Collins Cromley and Carter L. Hudgins (Knoxville, TN: University of Tennessee Press, 1995), 167-70.

103 King, *The Bungalow*, 265-7.

104 Marsan, *Montreal in Evolution*, 265-75.

105 O'Brien, *Journals of Mary O'Brien*, 191.

106 Quoted in Edwinna von Baeyer, *Rhetoric and Roses: A History of Canadian Gardening 1900-1930* (Toronto: Fitzhenry and Whiteside, 1984), 104.

107 Virginia Scott Jenkins, *The Lawn: A History of an American Obsession* (Washington, DC, and London, UK: Smithsonian Institution, 1994), 183-7.

108 Von Baeyer, *Rhetoric and Roses*, 4-9; Pleasance Crawford, 'The Ontario Home Landscape: 1890-1914' (Unpublished report prepared for the Department of Landscape Architecture, University of Toronto, 1981), 13.

109 Leonore Davidoff and Catherine Hall, *Family Fortunes: Men and Women of the English Middle Class, 1780-1850* (London: Hutchinson, 1987), 373-4.

110 Dianne Harris, 'Cultivating Power: The Language of Feminism in Women's Garden Literature, 1870-1920,' *Landscape Journal* 13, 2 (1994): 113-23.

111 Marion Roberts, *Living in a Man-made World: Gender Assumptions in Modern Housing Design* (London and New York: Routledge, 1991); Leslie Kanes Weisman, *Discrimination by Design: A Feminist Critique of the Man-Made Environment* (Urbana: University of Illinois Press, 1992); Pocius, *A Place to Belong*, 93.

112 Francesca Bray, *Technology and Gender: Fabrics of Power in Late Imperial China* (Berkeley, CA: University of California Press, 1997).

113 Elizabeth Collins Cromley, *Alone Together: A History of New York's Early Apartments* (Ithaca, NY, and London, UK: Cornell University Press, 1990).

Suggested Reading

Books about houses fill libraries, not just shelves. For this reason the following is just a short list of recommended starting points for a long, winding literary journey through the history of the house as a social place, in Canada and elsewhere.

In Canada the most obvious point of departure is Peter Ennals and Deryck Holdsworth's *Homeplace: The Making of the Canadian Dwelling over Three Centuries* (Toronto: University of Toronto Press, 1998), which appeared just as this book was going to press. Concerned with dwellings as physical and cultural objects more than as social spaces, it provides a fine complement to what I've written here. Donald G. Wetherell and Irene R.A. Kmet's survey, *Homes in Alberta: Building, Trends, and Design* (Edmonton: University of Alberta Press, 1991), explores the changing pattern of house design and construction as well as the economic and social dimensions of housing. Although it refers almost entirely to Alberta, it touches on broad themes in history of the modern Canadian home. Michael Doucet and John Weaver's weighty *Housing the North American City* (Montreal and Kingston: McGill-Queen's University Press, 1991) unravels many strands in the evolution of the dwelling, including land development, construction practices, home financing, property ownership, and the rise of apartment dwelling. While concerned with the North American pattern in its broadest sense, the authors employ Hamilton as a case study. Gerald L. Pocius's *A Place to Belong: Community Order and Everyday Space in Calvert, Newfoundland* (Montreal and Kingston: McGill-Queen's University Press, 1991) offers a finely grained portrait of spatial and social relations in a small Canadian community. Would that his work were duplicated elsewhere in the country. Among the many studies of early home interiors, Peter Moogk's 'At Home in Early Niagara Township,' *The Capital Years: Niagara-on-the-Lake, 1792-1796*, ed. Richard Merritt, Nancy Butler, and Michael Power (Toronto and Oxford: Dundurn Press, 1991), 165-85, is particularly informative. Harold Kalman's two-volume *A History of Canadian Architecture* (Toronto: Oxford University Press, 1994) incorporates housing within a much broader discussion of Canada's building history.

The Quebec dwelling has a particularly long history and, not surprisingly, a rich literature that explores it. Michel Lessard and Gilles Vilandré's encyclopaedic *La maison traditionelle au Québec* (Montreal: Les Éditions de l'homme, 1974) provides a feast of descriptive information about early Quebec dwellings, including numerous floor plans and extensive details about historical construction practices. Hélène Bourque's *La maison de faubourg: L'architecture domestique des faubourgs Saint-Jean et Saint-Roch avant 1845* (Quebec: Institut québécois de recherche sur la culture, 1991) discusses building types and construction processes in Canada's first suburbs. France Gagnon-Pratte's handsome exhibition catalogue, *L'Architecture et la nature à Québec au dix-neuvième siècle: les villas* (Quebec: Ministère des Affaires culturelles, 1980), includes numerous illustrations and many plans of nineteenth-century country homes in the vicinity of Quebec City. Jean-Pierre Hardy's essay 'Niveaux de richesse et intérieurs domestiques dans le quartier Saint-Roch à Québec, 1820-1850,' *Material History Bulletin* 17 (1983): 63-94 is a particularly useful survey of urban working-class home interiors in the first half of the nineteenth century. Jean-Claude Marsan's *Montreal in Evolution* (Montreal and Kingston: McGill-Queen's University Press, 1981) places the city's distinctive house types in the broader setting of its architectural history.

Elsewhere the literature on the history of the dwelling multiplies. The chapters on housing in Donald J. Olsen's evocative *The City As a Work of Art: London, Paris, Vienna* (New Haven and London: Yale University Press, 1986) piqued my early interest in dwellings and prompted me to think about the social history of the Canadian home. Witold Rybczynski's best-selling *Home: A Short History of an Idea* (New York: Viking Penguin, 1986) spans five centuries of domestic life in Europe and North America and discusses themes linked to those explored in this book. Though published three decades ago, Amos Rapoport's *House Form and Culture* (Englewood Cliffs, NJ: Prentice Hall, 1969) remains highly suggestive. It identifies the universal features of the dwelling in their various forms and seeks to explain what accounts for these variations.

James Ackerman's elegant overview of the villa in western history is particularly insightful: *The Villa: Form and Ideology of Country Houses*, The A.W. Mellon Lectures in the Fine Arts, 1985, Bollingen Series 35 (Princeton, NJ: Princeton University Press, 1990). *The Bungalow: The Production of a Global Culture*, 2nd ed. (New York, Oxford: Oxford University Press, 1995), by Anthony D. King, explores the history of a distinctive, yet pervasive, dwelling form with variants found in India, Great Britain, the United States, Canada, Australia, and Africa. Two works by Spiro Kostof provide useful, handsomely illustrated introductions to the broader study of urban form: *The City Shaped: Urban Patterns and Meanings through History* (Boston: Little, Brown, 1991) and *The City Assembled: The Elements of Urban Form through History* (Boston: Bullfinch Press, 1992).

Gwendolyn Wright's *Building the Dream: A Social History of Housing in America* (New York: Pantheon, 1981) remains the most accessible and reliable survey of the history of the American home. *The Comfortable House: North American Suburban Architecture, 1890-1930* (Cambridge, MA: MIT Press, 1986), by Alan

Gowans, discusses the first age of mass-produced housing in the United States, with an accent on stylistic matters. The most perceptive study of apartments and apartment life is Elizabeth Collins Cromley's *Alone Together: A History of New York's Early Apartments* (Ithaca and London: Cornell University Press, 1990). Henry Glassie's classic *Folk Housing in Middle Virginia: A Structural Analysis of Historic Artifacts* (Knoxville, TN: University of Tennessee Press, 1975) offers a broad interpretive framework for understanding the relationship between house form on one hand and domestic and community life on the other. A short essay by Dell Upton, 'The Traditional House and Its Enemies,' *Traditional Dwellings and Settlements Review* 1/2 (Spring 1990): 71-84, explores this theme further, at the same time providing an introduction to more recent writing about the American home as social space.

Leonore Davidoff and Catherine Hall's wide-ranging *Family Fortunes: Men and Women of the English Middle Class, 1780-1850* (London: Hutchinson, 1987) offers insights into middle-class English domesticity during the early industrial era, while M.J. Daunton's *House and Home in the Victorian City: Working-Class Housing, 1850-1914* (London: Edward Arnold, 1983) provides a comprehensive overview of housing conditions among British working families during the flood tide of industrialization. Two French studies complete this impressionistic list: Monique Eleb-Vidal with Anne Debarre-Blanchard, *Architectures de la vie privée: Maisons et mentalités, xviie-xixe siècles* (Brussels: Archives d'architecture moderne, 1989) and Monique Eleb with Anne Debarre, *L'invention de l'habitation moderne: Paris, 1880-1914* (Paris: Hazan et Archives d'architecture moderne, 1995). Together they survey the reshaping of domestic space in France from the *ancien régime* to the *fin de siècle*.

Illustration Credits

10 Plan for MacKearn and McEwan house, detail, Niagara-on-the-Lake, Ontario, National Archives of Canada RG19, E5(a), vol. 3471:61 / 27

11 Plan for Acacia Grove, detail, an early-nineteenth-century house at Starrs Point, Nova Scotia. From Arthur W. Wallace, *An Album of Drawings of Early Buildings in Nova Scotia* (Halifax: Heritage Trust and the Nova Scotia Museum, 1976), 47-9. Courtesy of the Nova Scotia Museum / 27

12 Drawing for G.W. Allan Mansion (Toronto, Ontario), to be erected on Wilton Crescent, plan of ground floor, Cumberland and Storm [between 1847 and 1855], J.C.B. and E.C. Horwood Collection C11-85-0, (90)32, Archives of Ontario / 28

13 Drawing for G.W. Allan Mansion (Toronto, Ontario), to be erected on Wilton Crescent, plan of upper floor, Cumberland and Storm [between 1847 and 1855], J.C.B. and E.C. Horwood Collection C11-85-0, (90)32, Archives of Ontario / 29

14 Drawing for G.W. Allan Mansion (Toronto, Ontario), to be erected on Wilton Crescent, plan of basement, Cumberland and Storm [between 1847 and 1855], J.C.B. and E.C. Horwood Collection C11-85-0, (90)32, Archives of Ontario / 30

15 Design for Dwelling Houses (Toronto, Ontario), Jarvis Street, plan of ground floor, Mathew Sheard, 1887, J.C.B. and E.C. Horwood Collection C11-658-0-1, (628a)9, Archives of Ontario / 32

16 Design for Dwelling Houses (Toronto, Ontario), Jarvis Street, plan of chamber floor, Mathew Sheard, 1887, J.C.B. and E.C. Horwood Collection C11-658-0-1, (628a)9, Archives of Ontario / 33

17 Design for Dwelling Houses (Toronto, Ontario), Jarvis Street, plan of attic floor, Mathew Sheard, 1887, J.C.B. and E.C. Horwood Collection C11-658-0-1, (628a)9, Archives of Ontario / 34

18 Sketch for Proposed Workmen's Dwellings (Location unknown), detail, W. Ford Howland and Burke and Horwood, 1905, J.C.B. and E.C. Horwood Collection C11-485-0-1, (454b)1-2, Archives of Ontario / 35

19 1937 housing survey showing typical single-floor dwellings. From Réal Bélanger, George S. Mooney, and Pierre Boucher, *Les vieux logements de Montréal* (Montreal: Commission métropolitaine de Montréal, Département d'urbanisation et de recherche, 1938) / 36

20 Plan for one-and-a-half storey house, 1919. From T. Eaton Company, *Plan Book of Ideal Homes* (Winnipeg: 1919), 8. Eaton Collection, Archives of Ontario / 39

21 Residence, Albert Street, Kingston, based on National Archives of Canada, Power Collection, 81203/19, project 1922-9, item 2, NMC161084 / 40

22 BC government plan for a bungalow farmhouse, 1916. From B.C. Dept. of Lands, Forest Service, *Farm Houses* (Victoria: William H. Cullin, King's Printer, 1916), 27 / 42

23 Plan for bungalow, detail, Kingston or area, 1946, based on National Archives of Canada, Power Collection, 81203/19, project 1946-27, item 1, NMC162597 / 43

24 Plan for row housing, detail, Saskatoon, 1968, based on National Archives of Canada, RG56M, 86703/31, item 4418, NMC162593 / 44

25 M.G. Angus residence, Westmount, Quebec, 1950, based on National Archives of Canada, H.L. Fetherstonhaugh Collection, 81203/1, job 5008, item 4, NMC160953 / 45

26 Demonstration home in White Rock, 31 October 1962, Vancouver Public Library, Special Collections, VPL 77564G / 46

27 Interior, John Beam's ranch house, north of Cochrane, Alberta, c. 1890, Glenbow Archives, Calgary, Canada NA-1130-9 / 50

28 Bathroom in house, Edmonton, 1914, Glenbow Archives, Calgary, Canada NA-1328-2645 / 59

29 William Topley, House interior for Mr. Lowe, Ottawa, 1890, National Archives of Canada C073321 / 63

30 Parlour of the Boose family home, near Vulcan, Alberta, 1910, Glenbow Archives, Calgary, Canada NA-1462-1 / 65

31 Mr and Mrs Hutchinson at home, Port Perry, Ontario, c. 1900, Archives of Ontario acc. 6989 s 12989 / 67

32 Edmund J. Massicotte, *Au foyer domestique,* 1900, National Library of Canada C14365 / 69

33 Unidentified adults and children, Toronto, c. 1890-1900, photographer: Arthur Beales, National Archives of Canada PA800199 / 69

34 Modern Canadian living room, 1956, photographer: C. Lund, National Archives of Canada PA111484 / 70

35 Gorsebrook, near Halifax, early nineteenth century, plan of ground floor. From Arthur W. Wallace, *An Album of Drawings of Early Buildings in Nova Scotia* (Halifax: Heritage Trust and the Nova Scotia Museum, 1976), 39-43. Courtesy of the Nova Scotia Museum / 75

36 Apartment kitchen, Montreal, c. 1947, National Archives of Canada PA160615 / 75

37 Modern Canadian kitchen, 1956, photographer: C. Lund, National Archives of Canada PA111483 / 76

38 Floor plan of apartment, detail, Winnipeg, 1961-2, National Archives of Canada, RG56M, 86703/31, item 6169, NMC162596-2 / 76

39 Mrs Arthur Beales in the kitchen of the Beales home, Toronto, c. 1903-13, photographer: Arthur Beales, National Archives of Canada PA800211, / 77

40 A. Muir, and Mrs Muir with their children in kitchen of old house in Cabbagetown, a slum district in the east end, Toronto, 1949 (Photographer: R. Beaver), National Archives of Canada PA111567 / 79

41 Substandard housing, Drumheller, Alberta, July 1966, Provincial Archives of Alberta PA 3667/4 / 79

42 Kitchen of summer home, Cooking Lake, Alberta, 1945, Provincial Archives of Alberta A 14166 / 80

43 Plan for Antoine Plamondon's house, Pointe aux Trembles, Quebec, 1846. From Yves Laframboise, *Neuville: Architecture traditionelle* (Quebec: Ministère des Affaires culturelles du Québec, 1976), 216 / 84

44 Drawing for eight-storey apartment building (Toronto, Ontario), detail, 195 Bloor St E at North St, Burke Horwood and White, 1910, J.C.B. and E.C. Horwood Collection C11-417-0-1 (1050) 25, Archives of Ontario / 85

45 Drawing for proposed apartment house building, detail, corner of Syden-

ham and William Streets, Kingston, 1928, based on National Archives of Canada, Power Collection, 81203/19, project 1928-8, item 13, NMC162600 / 86

46 Mrs Louise Watson in bedroom of 20 Carleton St, Toronto, c. 1910, Archives of Ontario S18227 / 87

47 Tenements for H[avelock] McColl Hart, detail, Lockman (Barrington) Street and Elevator Court, Halifax, NS, 1906, location 1.4.11.6, Nova Scotia Archives and Records Management / 91

48 Plan for two-bedroom one-level apartment, Strathern Heights, Edmonton, early 1950s, author's possession / 92

49 Plan of apartment house for Miss E. Hunter, detail, 42 Perrault St, Ste Anne de Bellevue, Quebec, 1953-4, based on National Archives of Canada, Dobush, Stewart, Hein Collection, 88921, project 53-19, item 1, NMC164164 / 92

50 The Regency, typical floor plan, detail, Edmonton, 1962, courtesy of John A. MacDonald, Edmonton / 94

51 Plan of apartment building for Centco Building Corporation, detail, Chouinard Street, Hull, 1971, based on National Archives of Canada, Bronson Collection, 79002/3397, item 56, NMC164165 / 95

52 Plan of circular apartment towers, detail, Frobisher Bay, 1958, National Archives of Canada RG11M, 83403/5, item 300, NMC122832 / 96

53 The Murray Map, detail, 1762, National Archives of Canada NMC10842 / 99

54 Homestead of Mr and Mrs Thomas Davis, Amaranth Township, Lot 21, Concession 8, 1900, Archives of Ontario acc. 6153 s 7991 / 101

55 Near Rowatt, Saskatchewan, July 1946, National Archives of Canada PA196507 / 102

56 Gilbert Berdahl farm, Hesketh, Alberta, 1960, Glenbow Archives, Calgary, Canada NA-2574-28 / 102

57 Hull ranch house, south of Calgary, 1895, Provincial Archives of Alberta P 309 / 104

58 Settlers' buildings and cattle on Bow River horse ranch near Cochrane, Alberta, c. 1890s, Glenbow Archives, Calgary, Canada NA-2084-40 / 104

59 Great Britain, Ordnance Survey, Plan of Kingston and its environs, Ontario, detail, 1869, National Archives of Canada NMC135768 / 106

60 George Heriot, *Monkville near Montreal*, 1813, National Archives of Canada Co10680 / 108

61 M.G. Hall, *View of Digby, Nova Scotia*, undated, National Archives of Canada Co04259 / 111

62 Looking north from King and York Streets, Toronto, 1856, City of Toronto Archives SC 498-16 / 113

63 Looking north from King and York Streets, Toronto, 1856, City of Toronto Archives SC 498-17 / 114

64 Scène de rue en hiver à Québec, 1872, photographer: L.-P. Vallée, National Archives of Canada PA103073 / 115

65 Quebec City, A street in old Sillery, c. 1900, Archives of Ontario F1075-9-0-8 s 8845 / 117

66 Typical late-nineteenth-century working-class Montreal streetscape. From Réal Bélanger, George S. Mooney, and Pierre Boucher, *Les vieux logements de Montréal* (Montreal: Commission métropolitaine de Montréal, Département

d'urbanisation et de recherche, 1938) / 118

Index

centre, 24, 25; and family room, 42; galley, 74; history of, 71-81; limited-purpose, appearance of, 73; modern, 74; open plan, 74; in row houses, 31; *salle commune* (Quebec), 25, 71; social functions of, 71-3; summer, 25, 71
Kostof, Spiro, 124

Lambert, John, 24
Lanes and alleys, 135. *See also* Streets
Large houses. *See* Historical houses; Houses; Wealthy
Laroque, Robert, 49
Lawns, front, 147-8
Lemoine, Julie, 18
Lighting: candles, 48; effect on social relations, 49, 51, 155; electric, 48-9, 51; history of, 48-51; kerosene lamps, 48, 49, *50;* oil lamps, 48
Lowe family, parlour of, *63*
Lower Canada. *See* Quebec
Lunenberg, Nova Scotia: grid design of streets, 124, *126-7;* housing conditions, 1891, 18-20; use of ceramic stoves, 47

MacDonald, John (Captain), 9-10
Maison Mourier (Ile d'Orléans, Quebec), 8-9
Mansions. *See* Historical houses; Wealthy
Maritime provinces: farmhouses, roadside, 100. *See also* names of individual provinces
Markus, Thomas, 3
Married couples: bedrooms, 81, 82, 87; and personal privacy, 154. *See also* Children; Courtship; Families; Women
Marsan, Jean-Claude, 140
Martin, Henry, *Plate 4*
Massicotte, E.J., 68, *69*
Maulson, John, 109
Military, and town planning, 120
Mill Woods (Edmonton, Alberta), 137, *138,* 139
Monk, James, 107
Monkville villa, 107, *108,* 140
Montebello (Petite Natione, Quebec), 17
Montreal, Quebec: apartments, 88, 89; balconies, 140; duplexes and triplexes, 31, 36, 90, 128; early industrial, people-to-room ratio, 18; early streetscapes, 110-1; electric lighting, 1937, 48; flush toilets, 52, 53; heating by cookstove, 1937, 47; historical houses, 41, *45,* 107, *108,* 140; house sizes (1860-1900), 14;

housing, history of, 14; interior baths, 58; row houses, 31, 112; single-family houses, lower percentage of, 129; single-floor dwellings, *36;* streets, grid plan, *121;* suburbs, 116, 120; verandahs, 142, 145; view from Citadel, *Plate 7;* villas, 105, 107, *108;* working-class housing, 116, *118,* 140
Montreal Sanitary Association, 57
Moody, John, 107
Mount Royal (Calgary, Alberta), 124
Mourier house (Ile d'Orléans, Quebec), 8-9
Murray, James (General), 98, *99*
Music making: decline of, in home, 68, 70; guitars, 68; pianos, 64-6, *65, 67*

New Brunswick, early rural kitchens, 72
Newfoundland: Calvert, bedrooms, 72, 83; Calvert, kitchens and social relations, 72, 136; Calvert, siting of houses for views, 136; tilt houses, 10
Niagara-on-the-Lake, Ontario, 124, *125*
Northern Canada, one and two-room houses, 11-3, *12*
Nova Scotia: Acadia, pioneer cabins, 9-10; early streetscapes, 111; historical houses, 17, 26, *27,* 73. *See also* names of specific cities and towns

O'Brien, Edward, 140
O'Brien, Mary. *See* Gapper, Mary
Odours: excretion, change in attitudes toward, 54-6; 'family,' and separate bedrooms, 83; food preparation, 74
O'Neill, Moira, 103, 105
Ontario: early house designs, 17-8, 25-6, *27;* early rural kitchens, 72; farmhouses, 100-1, *101;* historical houses, 26, *28, 29, 30,* 56, 66, 140, *146;* multiple-unit housing, 90; pioneer cabins, 10; suburbs, 109-10; town planning, and grid design, 124. *See also* names of specific cities and towns
Open plan design, 37-8, *42-5*
Ottawa, Ontario: back yards, 148, *149,* 150, *151;* Black family house, *143;* MacLaren Street, upper-class housing, 116, *119*
Overcrowding: Britain, late nineteenth century, 20; and poverty, 15, 155; and social conditions, 14, 15, 18-24

Papineau, Louis Joseph, 17
Paradis house (Charlesbourg, Quebec), 25, *25,* 83

Parlour (salon): history of, 60-71; in row houses, 31; as *salon*, in French-Canadian homes, 25, 61, 71; and status, 62-3; use of, 61-2, 71-2; and visitors, 60-1, 62. *See also* Pianos

Patios. *See* Verandahs, porches, patios, and decks

Pearce, William, 20, 21

Perkins, Simeon, 17

Perkins (Simeon) House (Liverpool, Nova Scotia), 17

Perrault, Joseph-François, 107

Perth, Ontario, housing conditions, 1891, 19, 20

Pianos: decline of popularity of, 68, 70; symbolism of, 63, 64-6, 70

Pioneer cabins: Nova Scotia, 9-10; prairies, 11; Quebec, 8-9; Upper Canada, 10, *11*. *See also* Farmhouses

Plamondon (Antoine) house (Pointe aux Trembles, Quebec), 17, 83, *84*

Pocius, Gerald, 72, 83, 136

Point Grey (Vancouver, British Columbia), 135-6

Point Levis, Plate 3

Pointe-Claire, Quebec, 120

Porches. *See* Verandahs, porches, patios, and decks

Poverty. *See* Overcrowding

Prairie provinces: farmhouses, 101, *102*, 103, *104*, 105; pioneer cabins, 11. *See also* names of specific provinces

Privacy: and bathrooms, 55-6, 60; and bedrooms, 81, 82; and curtains, as room partitions, 24, 81; and gardens, 145; and gender, 156-7; growth of, 156; and individualism, 160; meanings of, 4-6, 158-60; and multiple-occupancy buildings, 158-9; personal, 6, 49, 51; and siting of urban single-family houses, 133-4; and solitude, 153; and technology, 155, 156, 159-60. *See also* Social relations

Quebec City, Quebec: central heating, introduction of, 47; early streetscapes, 111; Faubourg Saint-Jean, *115*, 115-6; Faubourg Saint-Roch, 112, 124; and grid design of streets, 124; rue Saint-Augustin, 140, *141;* St Louis Street, Plate 8; Sillery area, 116, *117;* single-family houses, lower percentage of, 129

Quebec (province): apartments, for working-class, 90; apartments, prevalence of, 88-9; duplexes and triplexes, 31, 36, 90, 128; early rural houses, 25; farmhouses, 22-4, *23*, 98, *99*, 100; historical houses, *Plate 2*, 8-9, 17, 25, 62, 107; houses, roadside, 98, *99*, 100, *115*, 115-6; housing, history of, 8-9; Joliette, housing conditions, 1891, 19; large rural houses, space use of, 25; single-family houses, lower percentage of, 129; suburbs, 112, *115*, 115-6, 124; upper-class housing, 116, *117;* workers' housing, 1801, 14

Railway companies, and town planning, 124

Ranch houses. *See* Farmhouses

Renovations, and relationship between homes and inhabitants, 4

River Heights (Winnipeg, Manitoba), 129, *131*

Robertson, Mr, 142

Rooms: basement, 46; den, 41; dining room, 26, 31, 74, 87; drawing room, *Plate 2*, 26, 31, 87; family room, 41, 42, 46, *46;* formal, 25; Georgian plan, 26; library, 26, 87; living room, 41; people-to-room ratio, 1891, 19, 20, 21; recreation, 41, 46; servants, 26, 83, 154; study, 41. *See also* Bathrooms; Bedrooms; Houses; Kitchens; Parlour (salon)

Row houses: Great Britain, 31; lack of transitional zones, 133; Ontario, 90; room arrangements, variations, 135; Saskatoon, Saskatchewan, *44;* and setbacks, 112; Toronto, Ontario, *32-5*, 31

Ste-Anne-de-Bellevue, Quebec, *92*, 93

Saint-Jean suburb (Quebec City, Quebec), *115*, 115-6

St John, New Brunswick, 52

St Louis Street, Plate 8, 111, 140

Saint-Roch suburb (Quebec City, Quebec), 112, 124

Salle commune, 25, 71

Salon. *See* Parlour (salon)

Saskatchewan: farmhouses, *102;* Saskatoon row houses, *44*

Scotland, housing before Second World War, 15

Scully, Vincent, 37

Seigneurie of Beauharnois, *Plate 2*, 62

Servants: and personal privacy, 154; rooms, 26, 83, 154

Sewers, 52

Shaughnessy (Vancouver, British Columbia), 124

Shopping malls, 139
Sierich, Otto, 10
Sillery area (Quebec City, Quebec), 116, *117*
Slum dwellings: kitchens, *75, 76;* space
   restrictions, 22, *23;* Toronto, Ontario,
   early twentieth century, 22, *23*
Social relations: Calvert, Newfoundland,
   72, 83, 136; and changes in privacy,
   154; farmhouses, 103, 105, 157-8; and
   heating, 66, 68, *69,* 70; and house
   design, 134-5, 136-7, 139-40, 142, 145,
   158; and kitchen, 24, 25, 42, 71-3; and
   lighting, 49, 51, 155. *See also* Families;
   Privacy
Status. *See* Parlour (salon); Pianos;
   Wealthy
Stratford, Ontario, 120, *123*
Streets: early unplanned streetscapes,
   110-2, 120; grid plan, 120, *121, 122,* 124;
   non-gridded, and British garden city
   movement, 124, 128; and pedestrians,
   142. *See also* Automobile, effect of;
   Lanes and alleys
Suburbs: automobile, effect of, 137, 139,
   142; growth of, 112, 115-6, 120; house
   design, 41-2, 137; lack of transitional
   spaces, 158; street design, 124, 128; and
   tradition of villas, 109-10, 158; uniformity, and municipal siting regulations, 128-9, *130, 131*
Summer cottages: kitchens, 78, *80,* 81;
   and tradition of villa, 110
Summer kitchens. *See* Kitchens

Tanswell, Honorine, 62
Television: and family relations, 70-1; as
   home entertainment, 46
Tilt house, 10
de Tocqueville, Alexis, 160
Todd, Frederick, 147
Toilets. *See* Bathrooms
Toronto, Ontario: apartments, *85;* baths
   or showers, prevalence of, 58; central
   heating, 1934, 48; early streetscapes,
   112, *113, 114;* electric lighting, 1933, 48;
   inner city, early twentieth century, 22,
   23; municipal siting regulations, 129;
   row houses, *32-5,* 31, 112; sewers, 52;
   suburbs, 120, 129, *130;* toilets, flush, 52,
   53; toilets, outdoor, 53; verandahs, 142,
   145
Toronto Department of Health, 15
Town planning. *See* Streets
Townhouses, 132
Trees, as windbreaks, 100-1
Triplexes, 31, 36, 90

Ukrainian settlers, early housing, 11, 61
Upper Canada. *See* Ontario
Urban design. *See* Streets

Vancouver, British Columbia: non-grid-
   ded areas, 124; single-family houses,
   129; suburban expansion, 116; sub-
   urbs, 120; views, 135-6
Verandahs, porches, patios, and decks,
   139-45. *See also* Balconies, apartment
Victoria, British Columbia, 136
Views, and siting of house, 135-6
Villas, 105-10, 148, 158. *See also* Suburbs;
   Summer cottages
Visitors: and kitchen, 71-3; and parlour,
   60-1, 62

Watson, Louise, *87,* 87
Wealthy: and non-gridded street design,
   124, 128; and personal privacy, 154,
   155, 156; and size and spacing of
   houses, 15, 116; and views from house,
   136. *See also* Historical houses
Widows and widowers: housing of, 20-1;
   separate bedrooms for, 82
Wilton Crescent house. *See* Allan (G.W.)
   house (Toronto, Ontario)
Windsor Park (Edmonton, Alberta), 128
Winnipeg, Manitoba: apartment
   kitchens, 74; single-family houses,
   129; suburban expansion, 116
Wix, Edward, 10
Women: and gardening, 150, 152; and
   pianos, 64-6, *65, 67;* and privacy, 156-7;
   responsibility for house, 157. *See also*
   Children; Families; Kitchens; Married
   couples
Woolsey, John William, 15-6
Woolsey family: homes of, 15-6; people-
   to-room ratio, 18; portrait, *Plate 1;*
   sleeping arrangements, 82

Canadian vs
American homes.